The Latest NINJA Foodi SmartLid Cookbook

1500 Days Healthy & Delicious Recipes for Beginners in Pressure Cooking, Air Frying, Slow Cooking, Grilling, and Baking

Julie C. Steel

All Rights Reserved.

The content contained within this book may not be reproduced, duplicated, or transmitted without direct written permission from the author or the publisher. Under no circumstances will any blame or legal responsibility be held against the publisher, or author, for any damages, reparation, or monetary loss due to the information contained within this book, either directly or indirectly.

Legal Notice: This book is copyright protected. It is only for personal use. You cannot amend, distribute, sell, use, quote or paraphrase any part, or the content within this book, without the consent of the author or publisher.

Disclaimer Notice:

Please note the information contained within this document is for educational and entertainment purposes only. All effort has been executed to present accurate, up to date, reliable, complete information. No warranties of any kind are declared or implied. Readers acknowledge that the author is not engaged in the rendering of legal, financial, medical, or professional advice. The content within this book has been derived from various sources. Please consult a licensed professional before attempting any techniques outlined in this book. By reading this document, the reader agrees that under no circumstances is the author responsible for any losses, direct or indirect, that are incurred as a result of the use of the information contained within this document, including, but not limited to, errors, omissions, or inaccuracies.

CONTENTS

INTRODUCTION 8

Get the most of Your Ninja Foodi Smartlid 9

When Using the Ninja Foodi Smartlid 10

Breakfast 12

    Almond Quinoa Porridge 12

    Quinoa Protein Bake 12

    Sweet Potatoes & Fried Eggs 13

    Ham & Broccoli Frittata 13

    Savory Custards With Ham And Cheese 14

    Mediterranean Quiche 14

    Cranberry Vanilla Oatmeal 15

    Bacon And Gruyère Egg Bites 15

    Chilaquiles 16

    Egg Spinach Bites 16

    Homemade Vanilla Yogurt 17

    Kale-egg Frittata 17

    French Dip Sandwiches 18

    Hearty Breakfast Skillet 18

    Avocado Cups 19

    Cinnamon Roll Monkey Bread 19

    Pepperoni Omelets 20

    Sausage & Broccoli Frittata 20

    Cinnamon Crumb Donuts 21

    Peanut Butter Banana Baked Oatmeal 21

    Carrot Cake Muffins 22

    Baked Eggs In Mushrooms 22

    Breakfast Egg Pizza 23

    Paprika Hard-boiled Eggs 23

    Poached Egg Heirloom Tomato 23

Snacks, Appetizers & Sides 24

    Herbed Cauliflower Fritters 24

    Popcorn Chicken 24

    Herb Roasted Mixed Nuts 25

Zucchini Muffins 25

Cheesy Cauliflower Tater Tots 26

Zesty Brussels Sprouts With Raisins 26

Potato Samosas 27

Wrapped Asparagus In Bacon 27

Crispy Cheesy Straws 28

Horseradish Roasted Carrots 28

Dried Tomatoes 29

Broccoli Turmeric Tots 29

Caramelized Cauliflower With Hazelnuts 30

Jalapeno Salsa 30

Sweet Potato Gratin 31

Mexican Rice & Beans 31

Rosemary Potato Fries 32

Artichoke Bites 32

Parmesan Stuffed Mushrooms 33

Jalapeno Meatballs 33

Spinach Hummus 34

Glazed Walnuts 34

Green Vegan Dip 34

Apricot Snack Bars 35

Crab Rangoon's 35

Poultry 36

Crumbed Sage Chicken Scallopini 36

Slow Cooked Chicken In White Wine And Garlic 36

Turkey Croquettes 37

Chicken Burrito Bowl 37

Chicken With Mushroom Sauce 38

Chicken And Broccoli Stir-fry 38

Chicken Chickpea Chili 39

Turkey & Squash Casserole 39

Turkey Green Chili 40

Bacon Lime Chicken 40

Chicken Pasta With Pesto Sauce 41

Chicken Piccata 41

Mini Turkey Loaves 42

Chicken Stroganoff With Fetucini 42

Hainanese Chicken 43

Herby Chicken With Asparagus Sauce 43

Caprese Stuffed Chicken 44

Chicken With Bacon And Beans 44
Indian Butter Chicken 45
Spicy Chicken Wings 45
Chicken With Cilantro Rice 46
Italian Turkey & Pasta Soup 46
Riviera Chicken 47
Blackened Turkey Cutlets 47
Turkey & Cabbage Enchiladas 48

Beef, Pork & Lamb **49**

Pot Roast With Biscuits 49
Barbecue Pork Ribs 50
Greek Beef Gyros 50
Char Siew Pork Ribs 51
Korean Cabbage Cups 51
Mongolian Beef 52
Cheesy Ham & Potato Casserole 52
Butter Pork Chops 53
Honey Short Ribs With Rosemary Potatoes 53
Bacon & Sauerkraut With Apples 54
Skinny Cheesesteaks 54
Ground Beef Stuffed Empanadas 55
Gingery Beef And Broccoli 55
Crispy Roast Pork 56
Southern Sweet Ham 56
Pork Pie 57
One Pot Ham & Rice 57
Chunky Pork Meatloaf With Mashed Potatoes 58
Beef And Bell Pepper With Onion Sauce 58
Pepper Crusted Tri Tip Roast 59
Braised Lamb Shanks 59
Calzones With Sausage And Mozzarella 60
Ham, Ricotta & Zucchini Fritters 61
Braised Short Ribs With Creamy Sauce 61
Cuban Pork 62

Fish & Seafood **63**

Cod Cornflakes Nuggets 63
Shrimp Egg Rolls 63
Tuna Zoodle Bake 64
Caramelized Salmon 64

Seafood Gumbo	65
Pepper Smothered Cod	65
Coconut Shrimp	66
Mustard And Apricot-glazed Salmon With Smashed Potatoes	66
Classic Crab Imperial	67
Chorizo And Shrimp Boil	67
Mussel Chowder With Oyster Crackers	68
Steamed Sea Bass With Turnips	69
Penne All Arrabbiata With Seafood And Chorizo	69
Salmon With Dill Sauce	70
Sweet & Spicy Shrimp	70
Spicy Grilled Shrimp	71
Tilapia & Tamari Garlic Mushrooms	71
Buttered Fish	72
Crab Bisque	72
Salmon With Dill Chutney	73
Spiced Red Snapper	73
Panko Crusted Cod	74
Sesame Tuna Steaks	74
Salmon, Cashew & Kale Bowl	75
Tuna Patties	75

Vegan & Vegetable 76

Parsley Mashed Cauliflower	76
Red Beans And Rice	76
Southwest Tofu Steaks	77
Italian Spinach & Tomato Soup	77
Noodles With Tofu And Peanuts	78
Cheese Crusted Carrot Casserole	78
Leeks And Carrots	79
Mashed Broccoli With Cream Cheese	79
Pomegranate Radish Mix	79
Hot & Sour Soup	80
Roasted Squash And Rice With Crispy Tofu	80
Veggie And Quinoa Stuffed Peppers	81
Stuffed Mushrooms	81
Steamed Artichokes With Lemon Aioli	82
Veggie Potpie	82
Veggie Primavera	83
Maple Dipped Kale	83
Tomato Galette	84

Green Squash Gruyere 84
Cheese And Mushroom Tarts 85
Cauliflower Enchiladas 85
Whole Roasted Cabbage With White Wine Cream Sauce 86
Cheesy Chilies 86
Cheesy Spicy Pasta 87
Grilled Tofu Sandwich 87

Desserts 88

Créme Brulee 88
Coconut Cream "custard" Bars 88
Churro Bites 89
Raspberry Cheesecake 90
Sweet And Salty Bars 90
Cheat Apple Pie 91
Irish Cream Flan 91
Coffee Cake 92
Chocolate Walnut Cake 92
Chocolate Bread Pudding With Caramel Sauce 93
Mini Chocolate Cheesecakes 93
Vanilla Cheesecake 94
Spiced Poached Pears 94
Dark Chocolate Brownies 95
Apricots With Honey Sauce 95
Caramel Walnut Brownies 96
Cherry Pie 96
Moon Milk 97
Portuguese Honey Cake 97
Strawberry Crumble 98
Cherry Cheesecake 98
Gingery Chocolate Pudding 99
Cranberry Cheesecake 99
Chocolate Mousse 100
Gingerbread 100

INDEX 101

INTRODUCTION

Hi, I'm Julie, my husband and I live in New Zealand as a family, we met at a food photography show, got married and opened a restaurant together, he is a former nutrition teacher and his job is to write about Articles on food, cooking, and food nutrition, and I discovered my passion for cooking while studying abroad.

Perhaps our dear fans and friends can often see the recipes of various family delicacies shared by Charlie on the food blog website. Now we use books as a carrier to record various simple and delicious recipes in text form, so that more friends enjoying food.

Introducing the ultimate guide to unleashing the full potential of your Ninja Foodi SmartLid! Our cookbook features over 1500 mouth-watering recipes that take advantage of the innovative cooking features of the SmartLid, allowing you to cook delicious meals with ease.

From appetizers to entrees, soups to desserts, this cookbook has it all. With easy-to-follow instructions and beautiful photos, you'll be able to create restaurant-quality meals in the comfort of your own home. Plus, our recipes are designed to be healthy and nutritious, so you can feel good about what you're eating.

The SmartLid's unique features, including its pressure cooking, air frying, and slow cooking functions, make it a versatile tool in the kitchen. Our cookbook will help you unlock the full potential of these features, so you can cook a wide variety of meals without the need for multiple appliances.

So whether you're a busy parent looking to create quick and healthy meals for your family, or a seasoned cook looking to expand your culinary repertoire, our Ninja Foodi SmartLid Cookbook has everything you need to elevate your cooking game and impress your guests.

Get the most of Your Ninja Foodi Smartlid

Pressure Cooking: The pressure cooking function on the Ninja Foodi Smartlid allows you to cook food quickly and evenly under high pressure. This is perfect for cooking tougher cuts of meat or grains like rice, which can take longer to cook using traditional methods.

Air Frying: The air frying function on the Ninja Foodi Smartlid uses hot air to cook food, providing a healthier alternative to deep frying. This function is perfect for cooking crispy chicken wings, French fries, and other fried foods.

Slow Cooking: The slow cooking function on the Ninja Foodi Smartlid allows you to cook food over a longer period of time at a low temperature, which can help to infuse flavors into your dishes. This is perfect for cooking stews, soups, and chili.

Steaming: The steaming function on the Ninja Foodi Smartlid allows you to cook food using steam, which helps to retain moisture and nutrients. This function is perfect for cooking vegetables, seafood, and dumplings.

Searing: The searing function on the Ninja Foodi Smartlid allows you to quickly brown or sear meats before pressure cooking, which can help to lock in flavor and juices. This function is perfect for cooking steaks, pork chops, and chicken breasts.

Sauteing: The sauteing function on the Ninja Foodi Smartlid allows you to cook food quickly over high heat, which is perfect for browning meat, onions, and garlic. This function is perfect for making stovetop dishes like spaghetti bolognese or beef stroganoff.

Baking: The baking function on the Ninja Foodi Smartlid allows you to cook cakes, muffins, and other baked goods using the pressure cooking function. This function is perfect for making desserts or baking bread.

When Using the Ninja Foodi Smartlid

Here are some common problems and solutions that may be encountered when using the Ninja Foodi Smartlid:

Overcooking or undercooking: Make sure to follow the recipe and cooking time provided in the cookbook. Adjust the cooking time and temperature if needed based on your preferences and the quantity of food being cooked.

Uneven cooking: Try to distribute the food evenly in the cooking pot or basket, and avoid overcrowding. If necessary, stir or flip the food halfway through the cooking process.

Lid seal issues: Make sure the sealing ring is clean and properly seated in the lid. Check the float valve for debris or damage and make sure it moves freely. If there are any issues with the sealing, refer to the troubleshooting section of the user manual.

Burn message: This message indicates that the food has stuck to the bottom of the pot or basket, and the temperature is too high. Release the pressure, remove the lid, and carefully stir the food. If needed, add a bit of liquid to the pot or basket before resuming cooking.

Error messages: Refer to the user manual for specific error messages and their corresponding solutions. In general, turn off and unplug the unit, wait for it to cool down, and then check for any visible damage or debris. If needed, contact customer support for assistance.

By following these tips and troubleshooting steps, you can make the most out of your Ninja Foodi Smartlid and enjoy delicious and healthy meals with ease.

Breakfast

Almond Quinoa Porridge

Servings: 6
Cooking Time: 1 Minute
Ingredients:
- 1¼ cups water
- 1 cup almond milk
- 1½ cups uncooked quinoa, rinsed
- 1 tablespoon choc zero maple syrup
- 1 cinnamon stick
- Pinch of salt

Directions:
1. In the Ninja Foodi's insert, add all ingredients and stir to combine well.
2. Close the Ninja Foodi's lid with the pressure lid and place the pressure valve in the "Seal" position.
3. Select "Pressure" mode and set it to "High" for 1 minute.
4. Press the "Start/Stop" button to initiate cooking.
5. Now turn the pressure valve to "Vent" and do a "Quick" release.
6. Open the Ninja Foodi's lid, and with a fork, fluff the quinoa.
7. Serve warm.

Nutrition Info:
- InfoCalories: 186; Fat: 2.6 g; Carbohydrates: 4.8 g; Protein: 6 g

Quinoa Protein Bake

Servings: 4
Cooking Time: 30 Minutes
Ingredients:
- Nonstick cooking spray
- 1 cup white quinoa, cooked
- 3 egg whites, lightly beaten
- ½ tsp salt
- ¼ cup red bell pepper, chopped
- ¼ cup spinach, chopped
- ½ cup mozzarella cheese, grated

Directions:
1. Spray the cooking pot with cooking spray.
2. In a large bowl, combine all ingredients thoroughly. Pour into pot.
3. Add the tender-crisp lid and select air fry on 350°F. Bake 25-30 minutes until lightly browned on top and eggs are completely set.
4. Let cool a few minutes before serving.

Nutrition Info:
- InfoCalories 191, Total Fat 3g, Total Carbs 28g, Protein 13g, Sodium 441mg.

Sweet Potatoes & Fried Eggs

Servings: 4
Cooking Time: x

Ingredients:
- 2 large sweet potatoes, peel & cut in 1-inch cubes
- 1 tbsp. apple cider vinegar
- 1 ½ tsp salt, divided
- 3 tbsp. extra virgin olive oil, divided
- 1 cup red onion, chopped
- 1 cup green bell pepper, chopped
- 2 cloves garlic, diced fine
- ½ tsp pepper
- ½ tsp cumin
- ½ tsp paprika
- 4 eggs
- 2 tbsp. cilantro, chopped

Directions:
1. Add potatoes, vinegar, and one teaspoon salt to the cooking pot. Add just enough water to cover potatoes.
2. Secure the lid and set to pressure cooking on high. Set timer for 5 minutes. When timer goes off, use quick release to remove the lid. Potatoes should be slightly soft. Drain and set aside.
3. Add one tablespoon oil to the cooking pot and set to sauté function on medium heat. When oil is hot, add onions and bell pepper, cook about 5 minutes or until tender. Add garlic and cook 1 minute more. Transfer to a bowl and keep warm.
4. Add remaining oil to the pot. When hot, add potatoes, remaining salt, pepper, cumin, and paprika and decrease heat to medium-low. Cook, stirring occasionally, until potatoes are nicely browned on the outside and tender.
5. Stir in the onion mixture and create 4 "wells" in the mixture. Crack an egg in each one.
6. Secure the tender-crisp lid and set to air fryer function on 350°F. Bake until whites are set. Sprinkle with cilantro and serve.

Nutrition Info:
- InfoCalories 239, Total Fat 15g, Total Carbs 18g, Protein 8g, Sodium 982mg.

Ham & Broccoli Frittata

Servings: 6
Cooking Time: 30 Minutes

Ingredients:
- 1 tbsp. butter, soft
- 1 cup red pepper, seeded & sliced
- 1 cup ham, cubed
- 2 cups broccoli florets
- 4 eggs
- 1 cup half-n-half
- 1 cup cheddar cheese, grated
- 1 tsp salt
- 2 tsp pepper
- 2 cups water

Directions:
1. Use the soft butter to grease a 6x3-inch baking dish.
2. Place the peppers in an even layer on the bottom of the dish. Top with ham then broccoli.
3. In a mixing bowl, whisk together eggs, half-n-half, salt, and pepper.
4. Stir in cheese and pour mixture over ingredients in the baking dish. Cover with foil.
5. Pour 2 cups water into the cooking pot and place the rack inside.
6. Place the baking dish on the rack and secure the lid. Select pressure cooking on high and set the timer for 20 minutes.
7. When the timer goes off, release pressure naturally for 10 minutes, then quick release.
8. Remove the baking dish and let cool at least 5 minutes. With a sharp knife, loosen the sides of the frittata then invert onto serving plate. Serve immediately.

Nutrition Info:
- InfoCalories 401, Total Fat 29g, Total Carbs 9g, Protein 26g, Sodium 1487mg.

Savory Custards With Ham And Cheese

Servings: 4
Cooking Time: 40 Min

Ingredients:
- 4 large eggs
- 1 ounce cottage cheese; at room temperature /30g
- 2 serrano ham slices; halved widthwise
- ¼ cup caramelized white onions /32.5g
- ¼ cup half and half /62.5ml
- ¼ cup grated Emmental cheese /32.5g
- ¼ tsp salt /1.25g
- Ground black pepper to taste

Directions:
1. Preheat the inner pot by choosing Sear/Sauté and adjust to Medium; press Start. Put the serrano ham in the pot and cook for 3 to 4 minutes or until browned, turning occasionally.
2. Remove the ham onto a paper towel-lined plate. Next, use a brush to coat the inside of four 1- cup ramekins with the ham fat. Set the cups aside, then, empty and wipe out the inner pot with a paper towel, and return the pot to the base.
3. Crack the eggs into a bowl and add the cottage cheese, half and half, salt, and several grinds of black pepper. Use a hand mixer to whisk the Ingredients until co cheese lumps remain.
4. Stir in the grated emmental cheese and mix again to incorporate the cheese. Lay a piece of ham in the bottom of each custard cup. Evenly share the onions among the cups as well as the egg mixture. Cover each cup with aluminum foil.
5. Pour 1 cup or 250ml of water into the inner pot and fix the reversible rack in the pot. Arrange the ramekins on top. Lock the pressure lid in Seal position; choose Pressure, adjust to High, and set the timer to 7 minutes. Press Start.
6. After cooking, perform a quick pressure release. Use tongs to remove the custard cups from the pressure cooker. Cool for 1 to 2 minutes before serving.

Mediterranean Quiche

Servings: 6
Cooking Time: 45 Minutes

Ingredients:
- Nonstick cooking spray
- 2 cups potatoes, grated
- ¾ cup feta cheese, fat free, crumbled
- 1 tbsp. olive oil
- 1 cup grape tomatoes, halved
- 3 cups baby spinach
- 2 eggs
- 2 egg whites
- ¼ cup skim milk
- ½ tsp salt
- ¼ tsp pepper

Directions:
1. Select bake function and heat to 375°F. Spray an 8-inch round pan with cooking spray.
2. Press the potatoes on the bottom and up sides of the prepared pan. Place in the cooker. Secure the tender-crisp lid and bake 10 minutes.
3. Remove pan from the cooker and sprinkle half the feta cheese over the bottom of the crust.
4. Set cooker to sauté function on medium heat. Add the oil and heat until hot.
5. Add the tomatoes and spinach and cook until spinach has wilted, about 2-3 minutes. Place over the feta cheese.
6. In a medium bowl, whisk together eggs, milk, salt, and pepper. Pour over spinach mixture and top with remaining feta cheese.
7. Place the pan back in the cooking pot and secure the tender-crisp lid. Set temperature to 375°F and bake 30 minutes or until eggs are completely set and starting to brown. Let cool 10 minutes before serving.

Nutrition Info:
- InfoCalories 145,Total Fat 8g,Total Carbs 12g,Protein 7g,Sodium 346mg.

Cranberry Vanilla Oatmeal

Servings: 6
Cooking Time: 8 Hours

Ingredients:
- Nonstick cooking spray
- 1 ½ cups steel cut oats
- 4 ½ cups water
- 1 ½ tsp cinnamon
- 2 ½ tsp vanilla
- 1 ½ cups cranberries, dried

Directions:
1. Spray the cooking pot with cooking spray.
2. Add the oats, water, cinnamon, and vanilla and stir to combine.
3. Secure the lid and set to slow cooker on low heat. Set timer for 8 hours.
4. When timer goes off stir in cranberries and serve.

Nutrition Info:
- InfoCalories 250,Total Fat 3g,Total Carbs 51g,Protein 7g,Sodium 2mg.

Bacon And Gruyère Egg Bites

Servings:6
Cooking Time: 26 Minutes

Ingredients:
- 5 slices bacon, cut into ½-inch pieces
- 5 eggs
- 1 teaspoon kosher salt
- ¼ cup sour cream
- 1 cup shredded Gruyère cheese, divided
- Cooking spray
- 1 cup water
- 1 teaspoon chopped parsley, for garnish

Directions:
1. Select SEAR/SAUTÉ and set temperature to HI. Select START/STOP and let preheat for 5 minutes.
2. Add the bacon and cook, stirring frequently, about 5 minutes, or until the fat is rendered and bacon starts to brown. Transfer the bacon to a paper towel-lined plate to drain. Wipe the pot clean of any remaining fat.
3. In a medium bowl, whisk together the eggs, salt, and sour cream until well combined. Fold in ¾ cup of cheese and the bacon.
4. Spray egg molds or Ninja Silicone Mold with the cooking spray. Ladle the egg mixture into each mold, filling them halfway.
5. Pour the water in the pot. Carefully place the egg molds in the pot. Assemble pressure lid, making sure the pressure release valve is in the SEAL position.
6. Select PRESSURE and set to LO. Set time to 10 minutes. Select START/STOP to begin.
7. When pressure cooking is complete, natural release the pressure for 6 minutes, then quick release the remaining pressure by moving the pressure release valve to the VENT position.
8. Carefully remove the lid. Using mitts or a towel, carefully remove egg molds. Top with the remaining ¼ cup of cheese, then place the mold back into the pot. Close the crisping lid.
9. Select AIR CRISP, set temperature to 390°F, and set time to 5 minutes. Select START/STOP to begin.
10. Once cooking is complete, carefully remove the egg molds and set aside to cool for 5 minutes. Using a spoon, carefully remove the egg bites from the molds. Top with chopped parsley and serve immediately.

Nutrition Info:
- InfoCalories: 230,Total Fat: 18g,Sodium: 557mg,Carbohydrates: 2g,Protein: 16g.

Chilaquiles

Servings: 6
Cooking Time: 25 Minutes
Ingredients:
- 2 tablespoons canola oil
- 1 white onion, chopped
- 1 green bell pepper, chopped
- 2 cans red enchilada sauce
- 10 hard taco shells
- 6 eggs
- Kosher salt
- Freshly ground black pepper
- ½ cup crumbled cotija cheese
- 2 tablespoons minced cilantro
- 1 avocado, pitted, peeled, and thinly sliced

Directions:
1. Select SEAR/SAUTÉ and set to HI. Select START/STOP to begin. Let preheat for 5 minutes.
2. Add the oil, onion, and bell pepper. Cook for 5 minutes, stirring occasionally.
3. Reduce SEAR/SAUTÉ to MED and select START/STOP to continue cooking. Add the enchilada sauce and stir, cooking for 5 minutes until sauce thickens slightly. Coarsely crumble the taco shells into the pot, then stir.
4. Crack the eggs over the mixture in the pot, making sure they are evenly distributed across the surface. Season the eggs with salt and pepper. Close crisping lid.
5. Select BAKE/ROAST, set temperature to 350°F, and set time to 14 minutes. Select START/STOP to begin.
6. After 12 minutes, check eggs for doneness. It may be necessary to cook the eggs for up to an additional 2 minutes for the egg whites to completely set.
7. When cooking is complete, open lid and garnish the eggs with the cotija cheese, cilantro, and avocado. Serve.

Nutrition Info:
- InfoCalories: 298, Total Fat: 20g, Sodium: 806mg, Carbohydrates: 23g, Protein: 8g.

Egg Spinach Bites

Servings: 6
Cooking Time: 27 Minutes
Ingredients:
- 4 slices of bacon
- 1/2 cup lite coconut milk
- 1 cup Spinach cut up
- 6 eggs

Directions:
1. Place air crisper basket in the Ninja Foodi and place the bacon in it.
2. Secure the Ninja Foodi lid and Air Fry them for 10 minutes.
3. Transfer the cooked crispy bacon to a plate and keep them aside.
4. Whisk egg with spinach, coconut milk and crispy bacon in a bowl.
5. Divide this batter in a silicone muffin tray.
6. Set the trivet in the Ninja Food then place the muffin pan over the trivet and seal the lid.
7. Secure the Ninja Foodi lid and turn the pressure valve to the 'closed' position.
8. Cook the egg bites for 17 minutes for 325 °F on Bake/Roast mode.
9. Once done, remove the lid and remove the bites from the muffin tray.
10. Serve warm.

Nutrition Info:
- InfoCalories 211; Total Fat 18.5 g; Total Carbs 0.5 g; Protein 11.5 g

Homemade Vanilla Yogurt

Servings: 6
Cooking Time: 8 Hours

Ingredients:
- ½ gallon whole milk
- 3 tablespoons plain yogurt with active live cultures
- ½ tablespoon vanilla extract
- ½ cup honey

Directions:
1. Pour the milk into the pot. Assemble pressure lid, making sure the pressure release valve is in the VENT position.
2. Select YOGURT and set time to 8 hours. Select START/STOP to begin.
3. After the milk has boiled, the display will read COOL.
4. Once cooled, the unit will beep and display ADD & STIR. Remove pressure lid. Add the plain yogurt and whisk until fully incorporated. Reassemble pressure lid, making sure the pressure release valve is still in the VENT position.
5. When incubating is complete after 8 hours, transfer the yogurt to a glass container or bowl, cover, and refrigerate for a minimum of 8 hours.
6. Once the yogurt has chilled, stir in the vanilla and honey until well combined. Cover and place the glass bowl back in the refrigerator or divide the yogurt into airtight glass jars. The yogurt may be refrigerated up to 2 weeks.

Nutrition Info:
- InfoCalories: 286,Total Fat: 11g,Sodium: 133mg,Carbohydrates: 38g,Protein: 11g.

Kale-egg Frittata

Servings: 6
Cooking Time: 20 Min

Ingredients:
- 1 ½ cups kale; chopped /195g
- 6 large eggs
- ¼ cup grated Parmesan cheese /32.5g
- 1 cup water /250ml
- 2 tbsp heavy cream /30ml
- ½ tsp freshly grated nutmeg /2.5g
- cooking spray
- Salt and black pepper to taste

Directions:
1. In a bowl, beat eggs, nutmeg, pepper, salt, and cream until smooth; stir in Parmesan cheese and kale. Apply a cooking spray to a cake pan. Wrap aluminum foil around outside of the pan to cover completely.
2. Place egg mixture into the prepared pan. Add water into the pot of your Foodi. Set your Foodi's reversible rack over the water. Gently lay the pan onto the reversible rack.
3. Seal the pressure lid, choose Pressure, set to High, and set the timer to 10 minutes. Press Start. When ready, release the pressure quickly.

French Dip Sandwiches

Servings: 8
Cooking Time: 1 Hr 35 Min
Ingredients:
- 2 ½ pounds beef roast /1125g
- 2 tbsp olive oil /30ml
- 1 onion; chopped
- 4 garlic cloves; sliced
- ½ cup dry red wine /125ml
- 2 cups beef broth stock /500ml
- 1 tsp dried oregano /5g
- 16 slices Fontina cheese
- 8 split hoagie rolls

Directions:
1. Generously apply pepper and salt to the beef for seasoning. Warm oil on Sear/Sauté and brown the beef for 2 to 3 minutes per side. Set aside on a plate.
2. Add onions and cook for 3 minutes, until translucent. Mix in garlic and cook for one a minute until soft.
3. To the Foodi, add red wine to deglaze. Scrape the cooking surface to remove any browned sections of the food using a wooden spoon's flat edge; mix in beef broth and take back the juices and beef to your pressure cooker. Over the meat, scatter some oregano.
4. Seal the pressure lid, choose Pressure, set to High, and set the timer to 50 minutes; press Start. Release pressure naturally for around 10 minutes. Transfer the beef to a cutting board and slice.
5. Roll the sliced beef and add a topping of onions. Each sandwich should be topped with 2 slices fontina cheese.
6. Place the sandwiches in the pot, close the crisping lid and select Air Crisp. Adjust the temperature to 360°F or 183°C and the time to 3 minutes. Press Start. When cooking is complete, the cheese should be cheese melt.

Hearty Breakfast Skillet

Servings: 4
Cooking Time: 35 Minutes
Ingredients:
- ¼ cup walnuts
- 2 tbsp. olive oil
- ½ cup onion, chopped
- 4 cups Brussel sprouts, halved
- 2 cups baby Bella mushrooms, chopped
- ¼ tsp salt
- ¼ tsp pepper
- 1 clove garlic, diced fine
- 3 tbsp. chicken broth, low sodium
- 4 eggs
- ¼ cup parmesan cheese, grated

Directions:
1. Set to sauté on medium heat. Add walnuts and cook, stirring frequently, 3-5 minutes or until golden brown. Transfer to small bowl to cool.
2. Add oil and let it get hot. Once oil is hot, add onions and Brussel sprouts and cook 5 minutes, stirring occasionally.
3. Stir in mushrooms, salt, and pepper and cook 10-12 minutes until vegetables are tender. Add garlic and cook 1 minute more.
4. Pour in broth and cook until liquid has evaporated, about 3 minutes.
5. Make 4 "well" in vegetable mixture and crack an egg in each. Add tender-crisp lid and set to air fryer function on 350°F. Bake 8-10 minutes, or until whites are cooked through.
6. Chop the walnut and sprinkle over top with parmesan cheese and serve.

Nutrition Info:
- InfoCalories 261,Total Fat 18g,Total Carbs 14g,Protein 13g,Sodium 399mg.

Avocado Cups

Servings: 2
Cooking Time: 12 Minutes

Ingredients:
- 1 avocado, halved and pitted
- Black pepper and salt, as required
- 2 eggs
- 1 tablespoon Parmesan cheese, shredded
- 1 teaspoon fresh chives, minced

Directions:
1. Set a greased square piece of foil in "Air Crisp Basket."
2. Set the "Air Crisp Basket" in the Ninja Foodi's insert.
3. Close the Ninja Foodi's lid with a crisping lid and select "Bake/Roast."
4. Set its cooking temperature to 390 °F for 5 minutes.
5. Press the "Start/Stop" button to initiate preheating.
6. Carefully scoop out about 2 teaspoons of flesh from each avocado half.
7. Crack 1 egg in each avocado half and sprinkle with salt, black pepper, and cheese.
8. After preheating, Open the Ninja Foodi's lid.
9. Place the avocado halves into the "Air Crisp Basket."
10. Close the Ninja Foodi's lid with a crisping lid and Select "Bake/Roast."
11. Set its cooking temperature to 390 °F for about 12 minutes.
12. Press the "Start/Stop" button to initiate cooking.
13. Open the Ninja Foodi's lid and transfer the avocado halves onto serving plates.
14. Top with Parmesan and chives and serve.

Nutrition Info:
- InfoCalories: 278; Fat: 24.7g; Carbohydrates: 9.1g; Protein: 8.4g

Cinnamon Roll Monkey Bread

Servings: 8
Cooking Time: 20 Minutes

Ingredients:
- 4 eggs
- ¼ cup whole milk
- 1 teaspoon vanilla extract
- ½ teaspoon cinnamon
- Cooking spray
- 2 tubes refrigerated cinnamon rolls with icing, quartered

Directions:
1. In a medium bowl, whisk together the eggs, milk, vanilla, and cinnamon.
2. Lightly coat the pot with cooking spray, then place the cinnamon roll pieces in the pot. Pour the egg mixture over the dough. Close crisping lid.
3. Select BAKE/ROAST, set temperature to 350°F, and set time to 20 minutes. Select START/STOP to begin.
4. When cooking is complete, remove pot from unit and place it on a heat-resistant surface. Remove lid. Let cool for 5 minutes, then top with the icing from the cinnamon rolls and serve.

Nutrition Info:
- InfoCalories: 327, Total Fat: 12g, Sodium: 710mg, Carbohydrates: 46g, Protein: 7g.

Pepperoni Omelets

Servings: 4
Cooking Time: 5 Minutes
Ingredients:
- 4 tablespoons heavy cream
- 15 pepperoni slices
- 2 tablespoons butter
- Black pepper and salt to taste
- 6 whole eggs

Directions:
1. Take a suitable and whisk in eggs, cream, pepperoni slices, salt, and pepper.
2. Set your Ninja Foodi to "Sauté" mode and add butter and egg mix.
3. Sauté for 3 minutes, flip.
4. Lock and secure the Ninja Foodi's lid and Air Crisp for 2 minutes at 350 °F.
5. Transfer to a serving plate and enjoy.

Nutrition Info:
- InfoCalories: 141; Fat: 11g; Carbohydrates: 0.6g; Protein: 9g

Sausage & Broccoli Frittata

Servings: 10
Cooking Time: 25 Minutes
Ingredients:
- 1 tbsp. olive oil
- 1 lb. country-style pork sausage
- 4 cups broccoli florets
- 1 onion, chopped
- ½ tsp salt
- ¼ tsp pepper
- 14 eggs
- ½ cup milk
- 2 cups cheddar cheese, grated

Directions:
1. Select sauté function on med-high heat.
2. Add olive oil, once it's hot, add sausage, broccoli, onions, salt, and pepper. Cook, stirring frequently, until sausage is no longer pink. Drain the fat.
3. In a large bowl, whisk together eggs, milk, and cheese. Pour over sausage mixture.
4. Set cooker to bake function on 350 °F. Secure the tender-crisp lid and set timer to 20 minutes.
5. Frittata is done when eggs are set. Let cool 5-10 minutes before serving.

Nutrition Info:
- InfoCalories 374,Total Fat 27g,Total Carbs 4g,Protein 28g,Sodium 432mg.

Cinnamon Crumb Donuts

Servings: 6
Cooking Time: 10 Minutes

Ingredients:

- Butter flavored cooking spray
- ¼ cup Stevia, granulated
- 1 cup + 3 ½ tbsp. flour, divided
- ¼ tsp cinnamon
- ¼ cup butter, cut in cubes
- ½ cup Stevia brown sugar, packed
- ½ tsp salt
- 1 tsp baking powder
- ½ cup sour cream
- 2 ½ tbsp. butter, melted
- 1 egg, room temperature
- ½ cup Stevia confectioners' sugar
- ½ tbsp. milk
- ½ tsp vanilla

Directions:

1. Select air fryer function and heat cooker to 350°F. Spray a 6 mold donut pan with cooking spray.
2. In a small bowl, combine ¼ cup granulated Stevia, 3 ½ tablespoons flour, and ¼ teaspoon cinnamon.
3. With a pastry cutter, or fork, cut in the cold butter until mixture resembles coarse crumbs. Cover and chill until ready to use.
4. In a large bowl, stir together 1 cup flour, the Stevia brown sugar, salt, and baking powder.
5. In a separate bowl, whisk together sour cream, melted butter, and egg. Stir into dry ingredients just until combined.
6. Spoon dough into prepared pan. Sprinkle chilled crumb topping evenly over the tops.
7. Place the pan in the cooker and secure the tender-crisp lid. Cook 10-11 minutes or donuts pass the toothpick test. Cool in the pan 10 minutes then transfer to a wire rack.
8. In a small bowl, whisk together Stevia powdered sugar substitute, milk, and vanilla. Drizzle donuts with glaze and serve.

Nutrition Info:

- InfoCalories 250,Total Fat 18g,Total Carbs 21g,Protein 4g,Sodium 366mg.

Peanut Butter Banana Baked Oatmeal

Servings: 8
Cooking Time: 20 Minutes

Ingredients:

- Nonstick cooking spray
- 1 ½ cups oats
- 1/3 cup sugar
- ¾ cup almond milk, unsweetened
- 2 tbsp. coconut oil, melted
- 1 egg
- ½ cup peanut butter, no sugar added
- 1 tsp baking powder
- 1 tsp vanilla
- 1 banana, sliced

Directions:

1. Select bake function and heat to 350°F. Spray an 8-inch baking pan with cooking spray.
2. In a large bowl, combine all ingredients, except bananas, and mix until thoroughly combined. Pour into prepared pan in an even layer.
3. Layer the banana slices on the top and place in the cooker. Secure the tender-crisp lid and bake 20 minutes or until edges start to brown.
4. Carefully remove the pan from the cooker and let cool 10 minutes before slicing and serving.

Nutrition Info:

- InfoCalories 304,Total Fat 13g,Total Carbs 39g,Protein 11g,Sodium 118mg.

Carrot Cake Muffins

Servings: 12
Cooking Time: 30 Minutes
Ingredients:
- ¾ cup almond flour, sifted
- ½ cup coconut flour
- 1 tsp baking soda
- ½ tsp baking powder
- 1 tsp cinnamon
- ¼ tsp salt
- ¼ tsp cloves
- ¼ tsp nutmeg
- 2 eggs
- ½ cup honey
- 1 tsp vanilla
- ¼ cup coconut milk, unsweetened
- 2 tbsp. coconut oil, melted
- 1 banana, mashed
- 1 ½ cups carrots, grated

Directions:
1. Select the bake function and heat cooker to 350°F. Line 2 6-cup muffin tins with liners.
2. In a medium bowl, combine flours, baking soda, baking powder, cinnamon, salt, cloves, and nutmeg.
3. In a large bowl, beat eggs, honey, vanilla, and milk together until thoroughly combined.
4. Add the melted oil and mix well.
5. Add the banana and beat to combine. Stir in dry ingredients until mixed in. Fold in carrots.
6. Spoon into prepared muffin tins about ¾ full.
7. Place muffin tin, one at a time on the rack in the cooker and secure the tender-crisp lid. Bake 25-30 minutes, or until muffins pass the toothpick test.

Nutrition Info:
- InfoCalories 113,Total Fat 4g,Total Carbs 16g,Protein 1g,Sodium 196mg.

Baked Eggs In Mushrooms

Servings: 4
Cooking Time: 15 Minutes
Ingredients:
- 4 large Portobello mushrooms, rinse & remove stems
- 4 eggs
- 1 ½ tbsp. extra virgin olive oil
- ½ tsp salt, divided
- ½ tsp black pepper, divided

Directions:
1. Set to bake function on 450°F.
2. Rub mushrooms with oil and half the salt and pepper. Place on a small baking sheet, cap side down.
3. Carefully crack an egg into each mushroom and season with remaining salt and pepper.
4. Place sheet in the cooker and secure the tender-crisp lid. Bake 12-15 minutes, or until whites of the eggs are cooked through. Serve immediately.

Nutrition Info:
- InfoCalories 122,Total Fat 10g,Total Carbs 2g,Protein 7g,Sodium 363mg.

Breakfast Egg Pizza

Servings: 8
Cooking Time: 28 Minutes
Ingredients:
- 12 eggs
- 1/2 cup heavy cream
- 1/2 tsp salt
- 1/4 tsp pepper
-
- 8 oz sausage
- 2 cups peppers sliced
- 1 cup cheese shredded

Directions:
1. Heat peppers in a bowl for 3 minutes in the microwave.
2. Place air crisper basket in the Ninja Foodi and place the bacon in it.
3. Secure the Ninja Foodi lid and Air Fry them for 10 minutes.
4. Transfer the cooked crispy bacon to a plate and keep them aside.
5. Whisk eggs with salt, pepper, and cream in a bowl.
6. Pour this mixture in a greased baking pan.
7. Place the trivet in the Ninja Food cooking pot and set the baking pan over it.
8. Secure the Ninja Foodi lid and turn the pressure valve to 'closed' position.
9. Select 'Bake/Roast' for 15 minutes at 350 °F.
10. Once done, top the egg bake with cheese and peppers.
11. Broil this pizza for 3 minutes in the broiler until the cheese melts.
12. Serve warm.

Nutrition Info:
- InfoCalories 489; Total Fat 43.3g; Total Carbs 5g; Protein 22.2 g

Paprika Hard-boiled Eggs

Servings: 3
Cooking Time: 25 Min
Ingredients:
- 6 eggs
- 1 cup water /250ml
-
- 1 tsp sweet paprika /5g
- Salt and ground black pepper, to taste

Directions:
1. In the Foodi, add water and place a reversible rack on top. Lay your eggs on the rack. Seal the pressure lid, choose Pressure, set to High, and set the timer to 5 minutes. Press Start.
2. Once ready, do a natural release for 10 minutes. Transfer the eggs to ice cold water to cool completely. When cooled, peel and slice. Season with salt and pepper. Sprinkle with sweet paprika before serving.

Poached Egg Heirloom Tomato

Servings: 4
Cooking Time: 10 Min
Ingredients:
- 4 large eggs
- 2 large Heirloom ripe tomatoes; halved crosswise
- 4 small slices feta cheese
- 1 cup water /250ml
-
- 2 tbsp grated Parmesan cheese /30g
- 1 tsp chopped fresh herbs, of your choice /5g
- Salt and black pepper to taste
- Cooking spray

Directions:
1. Pour the water into the Ninja Foodi and fit the reversible rack. Grease the ramekins with the cooking spray and crack each egg into them.
2. Season with salt and pepper. Cover the ramekins with aluminum foil. Place the cups on the trivet. Seal the lid.
3. Select Steam mode for 3 minutes on High pressure. Press Start/Stop. Once the timer goes off, do a quick pressure release. Use a napkin to remove the ramekins onto a flat surface.
4. In serving plates, share the halved tomatoes, feta slices, and toss the eggs in the ramekin over on each tomato half. Sprinkle with salt and pepper, parmesan, and garnish with chopped herbs.

Snacks, Appetizers & Sides

Herbed Cauliflower Fritters

Servings: 7
Cooking Time: 13 Minutes
Ingredients:
- 1-pound cauliflower
- 1 medium white onion
- 1 teaspoon salt
- ½ teaspoon ground white pepper
- 1 tablespoon sour cream
- 1 teaspoon turmeric
- ½ cup dill, chopped
- 1 teaspoon thyme
- 3 tablespoons almond flour
- 1 egg
- 2 tablespoons butter

Directions:
1. Wash the cauliflower and separate it into the florets.
2. Chop the florets and place them in a blender.
3. Peel the onion and dice it. Add the diced onion to a blender and blend the mixture.
4. When you get the smooth texture, add salt, ground white pepper, sour cream, turmeric, dill, thyme, and almond flour.
5. Add egg blend the mixture well until a smooth dough form.
6. Remove the cauliflower dough from a blender and form the medium balls.
7. Flatten the balls a little. Set the Ninja Foodi's insert to" Sauté" mode.
8. Add the butter to the Ninja Foodi's insert and melt it.
9. Add the cauliflower fritters in the Ninja Foodi's insert, and sauté them for 6 minutes.
10. Flip them once. Cook the dish in" Sauté" stew mode for 7 minutes.
11. Once done, remove the fritters from the Ninja Foodi's insert.
12. Serve immediately.

Nutrition Info:
- InfoCalories: 143; Fat: 10.6g; Carbohydrates: 9.9g; Protein: 5.6g

Popcorn Chicken

Servings: 4
Cooking Time: 15 Minutes
Ingredients:
- Nonstick cooking spray
- 1 cup cornflakes, crushed
- ½ cup Bisquick baking mix, reduced fat
- ½ tsp garlic powder
- ½ tsp salt
- ¼ tsp pepper
- ½ tsp paprika
- ¾ lb. chicken breasts, boneless, skinless & cut in 1-inch pieces

Directions:
1. Lightly spray fryer basket with cooking spray.
2. In a large Ziploc bag, combine cornflakes, baking mix, garlic powder, salt, pepper, and paprika, shake to mix.
3. Add chicken and shake to coat.
4. Place chicken in basket in single layer, spray lightly with cooking spray.
5. Add the tender-crisp lid and set to air fry on 400°F. Cook chicken 12-15 minutes until crispy on the outside and no longer pink on the inside, turning over halfway through cooking time. Serve immediately.

Nutrition Info:
- InfoCalories 179,Total Fat 3g,Total Carbs 17g,Protein 21g,Sodium 596mg.

Herb Roasted Mixed Nuts

Servings: 12
Cooking Time: 15 Minutes
Ingredients:
- ½ cup pecan halves
- ½ cup raw cashews
- ½ cup walnut halves
- ½ cup hazelnuts
- ½ cup Brazil nuts
- ½ cup raw almonds
- 1 tbsp. fresh rosemary, chopped
- 1 tbsp. fresh thyme, chopped
- ½ tbsp. fresh parsley, chopped
- 1 tsp garlic granules
- ½ tsp paprika
- ½ tsp salt
- ¼ tsp pepper
- ½ tbsp. olive oil

Directions:
1. Combine all ingredients in a large bowl and toss to coat thoroughly.
2. Pour the nuts in the fryer basket and place in the cooking pot. Add the tender-crisp lid and select air fry on 375°F. Cook 10 minutes, then stir the nuts around.
3. Cook another 5-10 minutes, stirring every few minutes and checking to make sure they don't burn. Serve warm.

Nutrition Info:
- InfoCalories 229,Total Fat 21g,Total Carbs 7g,Protein 5g,Sodium 99mg.

Zucchini Muffins

Servings: 6
Cooking Time: 15 Minutes
Ingredients:
- 1 cup coconut flour
- 1 medium zucchini, finely chopped
- 1 teaspoon baking soda
- 1 tablespoon lemon juice
- ½ teaspoon salt
- ½ teaspoon black pepper
- 1 tablespoon butter
- ⅓ cup of coconut milk
- 1 teaspoon poppy seeds
- 2 tablespoons flax meal

Directions:
1. Place the chopped zucchini in a blender and mix until smooth.
2. Combine the salt, baking soda, lemon juice, poppy, coconut flour, butter, black pepper, and flax meal together.
3. Add the milk and blended zucchini.
4. Knead the dough until smooth. It can be a little bit sticky.
5. Place the muffins in the muffin's tins and transfer the zucchini muffins in the Ninja Foodi's insert.
6. Cook the muffins on the" Steam" mode for 15 minutes.
7. Once done, check if the dish is done using a toothpick.
8. If the muffins are cooked, remove them from the Ninja Foodi's insert and serve.

Nutrition Info:
- InfoCalories: 146; Fat: 8.9g; Carbohydrates: 13.5g; Protein: 4g

Cheesy Cauliflower Tater Tots

Servings: 10
Cooking Time: 35 Min

Ingredients:
- 2 lb. cauliflower florets, steamed /900g
- 5 oz. cheddar cheese /150g
- 1 egg, beaten
- 1 onion; diced
- 1 cup breadcrumbs /130g
- 1 tsp chopped chives /5g
- 1 tsp garlic powder /5g
- 1 tsp chopped parsley /5g
- 1 tsp chopped oregano /5g
- Salt and pepper, to taste

Directions:
1. Mash the cauliflower and place it in a large bowl. Add the onion, parsley, oregano, chives, garlic powder, salt, and pepper, and cheddar cheese. Mix with hands until thoroughly combined.
2. Form 12 balls out of the mixture. Line a baking sheet with paper. Dip half of the tater tots into the egg and then coat with breadcrumbs.
3. Arrange them on the baking sheet, close the crisping lid and cook in the Ninja Foodi at 350 °F or 177°C for 15 minutes on Air Crisp mode. Repeat with the other half.

Zesty Brussels Sprouts With Raisins

Servings: 4
Cooking Time: 45 Min

Ingredients:
- 14 oz. Brussels sprouts, steamed /420g
- 2 oz. toasted pine nuts /60g
- 2 oz. raisins /60g
- 1 tbsp olive oil/15ml
- Juice and zest of 1 orange

Directions:
1. Soak the raisins in the orange juice and let sit for about 20 minutes. Drizzle the Brussels sprouts with the olive oil, and place them in the basket of the Ninja Foodi.
2. Close the crisping lid and cook for 15 minutes on Air Crisp mode at 370 °F or 188°C. Remove to a bowl and top with pine nuts, raisins, and orange zest.

Potato Samosas

Servings: 4
Cooking Time: 31 Minutes

Ingredients:
- 2 tablespoons canola oil
- 4 cups Russet potatoes, peeled and cut into ½-inch cubes
- 1 small yellow onion, diced
- 1 cup frozen peas
- 1½ teaspoons kosher salt
- 2½ teaspoons curry powder
- 1 cup vegetable stock
- 1 (½ package) frozen puff pastry sheet, thawed
- 1 egg beaten with 1 teaspoon water

Directions:
1. Select SEAR/SAUTÉ and set temperature to HI. Select START/STOP to begin. Let preheat for 5 minutes.
2. Add the oil and let heat for 1 minute. Add the potatoes, onions, and peas and cook, stirring frequently, about 10 minutes. Add the salt and curry powder and stir to coat the vegetables with it. Add the vegetable stock. Assemble pressure lid, making sure the pressure release valve is in the SEAL position.
3. Select PRESSURE and set to LO. Set time to 1 minute. Select START/STOP to begin.
4. When pressure cooking is complete, quick release the pressure by turning the pressure release valve to the VENT position. Carefully remove the lid when the unit has finished releasing pressure.
5. Transfer the potato mixture to a medium bowl. Let fully cool, about 15 minutes.
6. Lay out the puff pastry sheet on a cutting board. Using a rolling pin, roll out the sheet into a 12-by-10-inch rectangle. Cut it in 4 strips lengthwise, then cut the strips into thirds for a total of 12 squares.
7. Place 2 tablespoons of potato mixture in center of a pastry square. Brush the egg wash onto edges, and then fold one corner to another to create a triangle. Use a fork to seal edges together. Repeat with the remaining potato mixture and pastry squares.
8. Insert Cook & Crisp Basket into unit. Close crisping lid. Select AIR CRISP, set temperature to 390°F, and set time to 20 minutes. Select START/STOP to begin. Let preheat for 5 minutes.
9. Once unit has preheated, working in batches, place 3 samosas in the basket. Close lid to begin cooking.
10. After 5 minutes, open lid and use silicone-tipped tongs to remove the samosas. Repeat with the remaining batches of samosas.
11. Once all samosas are cooked, serve immediately.

Nutrition Info:
- InfoCalories: 449, Total Fat: 24g, Sodium: 639mg, Carbohydrates: 53g, Protein: 10g.

Wrapped Asparagus In Bacon

Servings: 6
Cooking Time: 30 Min

Ingredients:
- 1 lb. bacon; sliced /450g
- 1 lb. asparagus spears, trimmed /450g
- ½ cup Parmesan cheese, grated /65g
- Cooking spray
- Salt and pepper, to taste

Directions:
1. Place the bacon slices out on a work surface, top each one with one asparagus spear and half of the cheese. Wrap the bacon around the asparagus.
2. Line the Ninja Foodi basket with parchment paper. Arrange the wraps into the basket, scatter over the remaining cheese, season with salt and black pepper, and spray with cooking spray. Close the crisping lid and cook for 8 to 10 minutes on Roast mode at 370 °F or 188°C. If necessary, work in batches. Serve hot!

Crispy Cheesy Straws

Servings: 8
Cooking Time: 45 Min
Ingredients:
- 2 cups cauliflower florets, steamed /260g
- 5 oz. cheddar cheese /150g
- 3 ½ oz. oats /105g
- 1 egg
- 1 red onion; diced
- 1 tsp mustard /5g
- Salt and pepper, to taste

Directions:
1. Add the oats in a food processor and process until they resemble breadcrumbs. Place the steamed florets in a cheesecloth and squeeze out the excess liquid.
2. Put the florets in a large bowl, and add the rest of the ingredients to the bowl.
3. Mix well with your hands, to combine the ingredients thoroughly.
4. Take a little bit of the mixture and twist it into a straw. Place in the lined Ninja Foodi basket; repeat with the rest of the mixture.
5. Close the crisping lid and cook for 10 minutes on Air Crisp mode at 350 °F or 177°C. After 5 minutes, turn them over and cook for an additional 10 minutes.

Horseradish Roasted Carrots

Servings: 4
Cooking Time: 10 Minutes
Ingredients:
- 1 pound carrots, peeled and cut into 1-inch pieces
- ½ cup vegetable stock
- 2 tablespoons grated horseradish
- ¾ cup mayonnaise
- ½ teaspoon kosher salt
- ½ teaspoon freshly ground black pepper
- Minced parsley, for garnish

Directions:
1. Place the carrots and stock in the pot. Assemble pressure lid, making sure the pressure release valve is in the SEAL position.
2. Select PRESSURE and set to HI. Set time to 2 minutes. Select START/STOP to begin.
3. When pressure cooking is complete, quick release the pressure by turning the pressure release valve to the VENT position. Carefully remove lid when unit has finished releasing pressure.
4. In a small bowl, combine the horseradish, mayonnaise, salt, and pepper. Add mixture to the cooked carrots and stir carefully. Close crisping lid.
5. Select BROIL and set time to 6 minutes. Select START/STOP to begin.
6. After 3 minutes, open lid to check doneness. If further browning desired, close lid and continue cooking.
7. When cooking is complete, garnish with parsley and serve immediately.

Nutrition Info:
- InfoCalories: 323, Total Fat: 30g, Sodium: 632mg, Carbohydrates: 13g, Protein: 1g.

Dried Tomatoes

Servings: 8
Cooking Time: 8 Hours

Ingredients:
- 5 medium tomatoes
- 1 tablespoon basil
- 1 teaspoon cilantro, chopped
- 1 tablespoon onion powder
- 5 tablespoon olive oil
- 1 teaspoon paprika

Directions:
1. Wash the tomatoes and slice them.
2. Combine the cilantro, basil, and paprika together and stir well.
3. Place the sliced tomatoes in the Ninja Foodi's insert and sprinkle them with the spice mixture.
4. Add olive oil and Close the Ninja Foodi's lid. Cook the dish on the "Slow Cook" mode for 8 hours.
5. Once done, the tomatoes should be semi-dry.
6. Remove them from the Ninja Foodi's insert.
7. Serve the dish warm or keep it in the refrigerator.

Nutrition Info:
- InfoCalories: 92; Fat: 8.6g; Carbohydrates: 3.84g; Protein: 1g

Broccoli Turmeric Tots

Servings: 8
Cooking Time: 8 Minutes

Ingredients:
- 1-pound broccoli
- 3 cups of water
- 1 teaspoon salt
- 1 egg
- 1 cup pork rind
- ½ teaspoon paprika
- 1 tablespoon turmeric
- ⅓ cup almond flour
- 2 tablespoons olive oil

Directions:
1. Wash the broccoli and chop it roughly.
2. Put the broccoli in the Ninja Foodi's insert and add water.
3. Set the Ninja Foodi's insert to "Steam" mode and steam the broccoli for 20 minutes.
4. Remove the broccoli from the Ninja Foodi's insert and let it cool.
5. Transfer the broccoli to a blender. Add egg, salt, paprika, turmeric, and almond flour.
6. Blend the mixture until smooth. Add pork rind and blend the broccoli mixture for 1 minute more.
7. Pour the olive oil in the Ninja Foodi's insert.
8. Form the medium tots from the broccoli mixture and transfer them to the Ninja Foodi's insert.
9. Set the Ninja Foodi's insert to "Sauté" mode and cook for 4 minutes on each side.
10. Once the dish is done, remove the broccoli tots from the Ninja Foodi's insert.
11. Allow them to rest before serving.

Nutrition Info:
- InfoCalories: 147; Fat: 9.9g; Carbohydrates: 4.7g; Protein: 11.6g

Caramelized Cauliflower With Hazelnuts

Servings: 4
Cooking Time: 15 Minutes
Ingredients:
- 1 head cauliflower, cut in ½-inch thick slices
- 2 cups cold water
- 2 tbsp. olive oil
- 1 tbsp. honey
- ½ tsp fresh lemon juice
- ½ tsp salt
- ¼ tsp pepper
- 1 tbsp. fresh sage, chopped
- 1 tbsp. hazelnuts, toasted & chopped
- ¼ cup parmesan cheese, reduced fat

Directions:
1. Remove any core from the cauliflower slices. Lay them in a single layer in the cooking pot.
2. Add enough water to come halfway up the sides of the cauliflower. Add oil, honey, lemon, salt, and pepper.
3. Set cooker to sauté on high. Cover and cook cauliflower until the water has evaporated, about 6-8 minutes. When it begins to brown reduce heat to low.
4. Once water has evaporated, flip cauliflower over and cook another 5 minutes, or until bottom is golden brown.
5. Transfer to serving plates and top with sage, hazelnuts, and parmesan cheese. Serve.

Nutrition Info:
- InfoCalories 112,Total Fat 8g,Total Carbs 9g,Protein 3g,Sodium 407mg.

Jalapeno Salsa

Servings: 10
Cooking Time: 7 Minutes
Ingredients:
- 8 ounces jalapeno pepper
- ¼ cup Erythritol
- 5 tablespoon water
- 2 tablespoons butter
- 1 teaspoon paprika

Directions:
1. Wash the jalapeno pepper and remove the seeds.
2. Slice it into thin circles. Sprinkle the sliced jalapeno pepper with paprika and Erythritol.
3. Put the butter and jalaeno mixture into the Ninja Foodi's insert and add water.
4. Set the Ninja Foodi's insert to" Sauté" mode.
5. Once the butter melts, add the sliced jalapeno in the Ninja Foodi's insert.
6. Close the Ninja Foodi's lid and sauté the dish for 7 minutes.
7. Once done, remove the dish from the Ninja Foodi's insert.
8. Cool it and serve.

Nutrition Info:
- InfoCalories: 28; Fat: 2.5g; Carbohydrates: 7.5g; Protein: 0.4g

Sweet Potato Gratin

Servings: 6
Cooking Time: 15 Minutes
Ingredients:
- 2 tablespoons unsalted butter
- 3 tablespoons all-purpose flour
- 2 cups heavy (whipping) cream, warmed in microwave
- 2 teaspoons kosher salt
- 1 teaspoon pumpkin pie spice
- ¼ cup water
- 3 large sweet potatoes, peeled and cut in half, then cut into half-moons ¼-inch thick
- 1¼ cups shredded Cheddar cheese, divided
- ½ cup chopped walnuts or pecans, or slivered almonds

Directions:
1. Select SEAR/SAUTÉ and set to MD:HI. Select START/STOP to begin. Let preheat for 5 minutes.
2. Add the butter. Once melted, add the flour and stir together until a thick paste forms, about 1 minute. (The combination of butter and flour is called a roux). Continue cooking the roux for 2 minutes, stirring frequently with a rubber-coated whisk. Slowly add the warm cream while continuously whisking so there are no lumps, about 3 minutes. The cream should be thickened.
3. Add the salt and pumpkin pie spice and whisk to incorporate. Whisk in the water and let the mixture simmer for 3 minutes.
4. Place the potatoes in the pot. Assemble pressure lid, making sure the pressure release valve is in the SEAL position.
5. Select PRESSURE and set to LO. Set time to 1 minute. Select START/STOP to begin.
6. When pressure cooking is complete, quick release pressure by moving the pressure release valve to the VENT position. Carefully remove lid when unit has finished releasing pressure.
7. Add ¼ cup of cheese and stir gently to incorporate, being careful not to break up the cooked potatoes. Ensure mixture is flat, then cover top with remaining 1 cup of cheese. Sprinkle the nuts over the cheese. Close crisping lid.
8. Select BROIL and set time to 5 minutes. Select START/STOP to begin.
9. When cooking is complete, open lid and let the gratin cool for 10 minutes before serving.

Nutrition Info:
- InfoCalories: 536, Total Fat: 47g, Sodium: 409mg, Carbohydrates: 20g, Protein: 10g.

Mexican Rice & Beans

Servings: 4
Cooking Time: 3 Hours
Ingredients:
- 1 cup rice, rinsed
- 1 jar salsa
- 1 can black beans, drained & rinsed
- 1 packet taco seasoning
- 1 cup vegetable broth
- 2 cloves garlic, diced fine
- 1 jalapeno, seeded & chopped

Directions:
1. Place all ingredients in the cooking pot and stir to mix.
2. Add the lid and select slow cooking on high. Set timer for 3 hours.
3. Cook until rice is tender and dip is heated through. Stir well then serve immediately.

Nutrition Info:
- InfoCalories 274, Total Fat 2g, Total Carbs 56g, Protein 9g, Sodium 1462mg.

Rosemary Potato Fries

Servings: 4
Cooking Time: 30 Min
Ingredients:
- 4 russet potatoes, cut into sticks
- 2 garlic cloves, crushed
- 2 tbsp butter, melted /30ml
- 1 tsp fresh rosemary; chopped /5g
- Salt and pepper, to taste

Directions:
1. Add butter, garlic, salt, and pepper to a bowl; toss until the sticks are well-coated. Lay the potato sticks into the Ninja Foodi's basket. Close the crisping lid and cook for 15 minutes at 370 °F or 188°C. Shake the potatoes every 5 minutes.
2. Once ready, check to ensure the fries are golden and crispy all over if not, return them to cook for a few minutes.
3. Divide standing up between metal cups lined with nonstick baking paper, and serve sprinkled with rosemary.

Artichoke Bites

Servings: 8
Cooking Time: 70 Min
Ingredients:
- ¼ cup frozen chopped kale /32.5g
- ¼ cup finely chopped artichoke hearts /32.5g
- ¼ cup goat cheese /32.5g
- ¼ cup ricotta cheese /32.5g
- 4 sheets frozen phyllo dough, thawed
- 1 lemon, zested
- 1 large egg white
- 1 tbsp olive oil /15ml
- 2 tbsps grated Parmesan cheese /30ml
- 1 tsp dried basil /5g
- ½ tsp salt /2.5g
- ½ tsp freshly ground black pepper /2.5g

Directions:
1. In a bowl, mix the kale, artichoke hearts, ricotta cheese, parmesan cheese, goat cheese, egg white, basil, lemon zest, salt, and pepper. Put the Crisping Basket in the pot. Close the crisping lid, choose Air Crisp, set the temperature to 375°F or 191°C, and the time to 5 minutes; press Start/Stop.
2. Then, place a phyllo sheet on a clean flat surface. Brush with olive oil, place a second phyllo sheet on the first, and brush with oil. Continue layering to form a pile of four oiled sheets.
3. Working from the short side, cut the phyllo sheets into 8 strips. Cut the strips in half to form 16 strips.
4. Spoon 1 tbsp of filling onto one short side of every strip. Fold a corner to cover the filling to make a triangle; continue repeatedly folding to the end of the strip, creating a triangle-shaped phyllo packet. Repeat the process with the other phyllo bites.
5. Open the crisping lid and place half of the pastry in the basket in a single layer. Close the lid, Choose Air Crisp, set the temperature to 350°F or 177°C, and the timer to 12 minutes; press Start/Stop.
6. After 6 minutes, open the lid, and flip the bites. Return the basket to the pot and close the lid to continue baking. When ready, take out the bites into a plate. Serve warm.

Parmesan Stuffed Mushrooms

Servings: 5
Cooking Time: 15 Minutes
Ingredients:
- 1 lb. button mushrooms, wash & remove stems
- 2 tbsp. olive oil, divided
- ¼ cup parmesan cheese, fat free
- 2 cloves garlic, diced fine
- ¼ cup cream cheese, fat free, soft
- ¼ cup whole wheat panko bread crumbs

Directions:
1. Place the rack in the cooking pot and top with a piece of parchment paper.
2. Brush the mushrooms with 1 tablespoon oil.
3. In a small bowl, combine parmesan, garlic, and cream cheese until smooth. Spoon 1 teaspoon of the mixture into each mushroom. Place mushrooms on parchment paper.
4. In a separate small bowl, stir together bread crumbs and remaining oil. Sprinkle over tops of mushrooms.
5. Add the tender-crisp lid and select bake on 375°F. Cook mushrooms 15 minutes, or until tops are nicely browned and mushrooms are tender. Serve immediately.

Nutrition Info:
- InfoCalories 121,Total Fat 6g,Total Carbs 10g,Protein 7g,Sodium 191mg.

Jalapeno Meatballs

Servings: 8
Cooking Time: 10 Minutes
Ingredients:
- 1 lb. lean ground beef
- ¾ lb. ground pork
- ½ cup panko bread crumbs
- 1 egg, beaten
- 2 tbsp. jalapenos, diced fine
- 1¼ tsp cumin
- 1 onion, grated
- 28 oz. tomatoes, crushed
- ½ cup fresh cilantro, chopped fine
- 2 tsp garlic, diced fine
- 1 tsp red pepper flakes
- ½ tsp cinnamon

Directions:
1. In a large bowl, combine beef, pork, bread crumbs, egg, jalapeno, cumin, and cinnamon. Mix well then form into meatballs.
2. Add the onion, tomatoes, cilantro, garlic, and red pepper flakes to the cooking pot. Place the meatballs in the sauce.
3. Add the lid and select pressure cooking on low. Set the timer for 10 minutes. When the timer goes off, use quick release to remove the lid.
4. Transfer meatballs to serving plate and top with sauce. Serve immediately.

Nutrition Info:
- InfoCalories 412,Total Fat 22g,Total Carbs 14g,Protein 38g,Sodium 320mg.

Spinach Hummus

Servings: 12
Cooking Time: 1 Hr 10 Min
Ingredients:
- 2 cups spinach; chopped /260g
- ½ cup tahini /65g
- 2 cups dried chickpeas /260g
- 8 cups water /2000ml
-
- 5 garlic cloves, crushed
- 5 tbsp grapeseed oil /75ml
- 2 tsp salt; divided /10g
- 5 tbsp lemon juice /75ml

Directions:
1. In the pressure cooker, mix 2 tbsp oil, water, 1 tsp or 5g salt, and chickpeas. Seal the pressure lid, choose Pressure, set to High, and set the timer to 35 minutes. Press Start. When ready, release the pressure quickly. In a small bowl, reserve ½ cup of the cooking liquid and drain chickpeas.
2. Mix half the reserved cooking liquid and chickpeas in a food processor and puree until no large chickpeas remain; add remaining cooking liquid, spinach, lemon juice, remaining tsp salt, garlic, and tahini.
3. Process hummus for 8 minutes until smooth. Stir in the remaining 3 tbsp or 45ml of olive oil before serving.

Glazed Walnuts

Servings: 4
Cooking Time: 4 Minutes
Ingredients:
- ⅓ cup of water
- 6 ounces walnuts
- 5 tablespoon Erythritol
-
- ½ teaspoon ground ginger
- 3 tablespoons psyllium husk powder

Directions:
1. Combine Erythritol and water together in a mixing bowl.
2. Add ground ginger and stir the mixture until the erythritol is dissolved.
3. Transfer the walnuts to the Ninja Foodi's insert and add sweet liquid.
4. Close the Ninja Foodi's lid and cook the dish in the "Pressure" mode for 4 minutes.
5. Remove the walnuts from the Ninja Foodi's insert.
6. Dip the walnuts in the Psyllium husk powder and serve.

Nutrition Info:
- InfoCalories: 286; Fat: 25.1g; Carbohydrates: 10.4g; Protein: 10.3g

Green Vegan Dip

Servings: 4
Cooking Time: 20 Min
Ingredients:
- 10 ounces canned green chiles, drained with liquid reserved /300g
- 2 cups broccoli florets /260g
- ¼ cup raw cashews /32.5g
- ¼ cup soy sauce /62.5ml
-
- 1 cup water /250ml
- ¾ cup green bell pepper; chopped /98g
- ¼ tsp garlic powder /1.25g
- ½ tsp sea salt /2.5g
- ¼ tsp chili powder /1.25g

Directions:
1. In the cooker, add cashews, broccoli, green bell pepper, and water. Seal the pressure lid, choose Pressure, set to High, and set the timer to 5 minutes. Press Start. When ready, release the pressure quickly.
2. Drain water from the pot; add reserved liquid from canned green chilies, sea salt, garlic powder, chili powder, soy sauce, and cumin.
3. Use an immersion blender to blend the mixture until smooth; set aside in a mixing bowl. Stir green chilies through the dip; add your desired optional additions.

Apricot Snack Bars

Servings: 16
Cooking Time: 25 Minutes

Ingredients:
- Butter flavored cooking spray
- ¾ cup oats
- ¾ cup flour
- ¼ cup brown sugar
- ¾ tsp vanilla
- ¼ cup butter
- ¾ cup apricot preserves, sugar free

Directions:
1. Lightly spray an 8-inch baking pan with cooking spray. Place the rack in the cooking pot.
2. In a large bowl, combine oats, flour, sugar, and vanilla until combined.
3. With a pastry blender or a fork, cut the butter in until mixture is crumbly. Press half the mixture in the bottom of the pan.
4. Spread the preserves over the top of the oat mixture and sprinkle the remaining oat over the top, gently press down.
5. Place the pan on the rack and add the tender-crisp lid. Set to air fry on 350°F. Bake 25-30 minutes until golden brown and bubbly.
6. Transfer to a wire rack and let cool before cutting.

Nutrition Info:
- InfoCalories 100,Total Fat 3g,Total Carbs 18g,Protein 2g,Sodium 3mg.

Crab Rangoon's

Servings: 15
Cooking Time: 20 Minutes

Ingredients:
- Nonstick cooking spray
- 8 oz. cream cheese, reduced fat, soft
- 1 tsp garlic powder
- 2 cups crab meat, chopped
- ¼ cup green onion, sliced thin
- 30 wonton wrappers

Directions:
1. Lightly spray the fryer basket with cooking spray.
2. In a medium bowl, beat cream cheese and garlic powder until smooth.
3. Stir in crab and onions and mix well.
4. Spoon a teaspoon of crab mixture in the center of each wrapper. Lightly brush edges with water and fold in half. Press edges to seal and lay in a single layer of the basket.
5. Add the tender-crisp lid and set to air fry on 350°F. Bake 15-20 minutes until crisp and golden brown, turning over halfway through cooking time. Serve immediately.

Nutrition Info:
- InfoCalories 236,Total Fat 3g,Total Carbs 15g,Protein 11g,Sodium 416mg.

Poultry

Crumbed Sage Chicken Scallopini

Servings: 4
Cooking Time: 12 Min
Ingredients:
- 4 chicken breasts; skinless and boneless
- 2 oz. flour /60g
- 3 oz. breadcrumbs /90g
- 2 eggs, beaten
- 2 tbsp grated Parmesan cheese /30g
- 1 tbsp fresh; chopped sage /15g
- Cooking spray

Directions:
1. Place some plastic wrap underneath and on top of the chicken breasts. Using a rolling pin beat the meat until it becomes fragile.
2. In a small bowl, combine the Parmesan, sage, and breadcrumbs. Dip the chicken in the egg first, and then in the sage mixture.
3. Spray with cooking oil and arrange the meat in the Foodi. Cook for 7 minutes on Air Crisp mode at 370 °F or 188°C.

Slow Cooked Chicken In White Wine And Garlic

Servings: 6
Cooking Time: 4 Hours
Ingredients:
- 6 bone-in, skin-on, chicken thighs
- 10 garlic cloves, peeled
- 6 cups chicken broth
- 1 cup dry white wine
- 2 teaspoons dried oregano
- 2 teaspoons kosher salt
- 1 teaspoon freshly ground black pepper
- ¼ cup capers, drained
- 1 tablespoon chopped fresh parsley

Directions:
1. Place the chicken, garlic cloves, chicken broth, wine, oregano, salt, and pepper in the cooking pot.
2. Assemble pressure lid, making sure the pressure release valve is in the VENT position. Select SLOW COOK and set to HI. Set time to 4 hours. Select START/STOP to begin.
3. When cooking is complete, carefully remove the lid. Stir in the capers.
4. Serve garnished with fresh parsley.

Nutrition Info:
- InfoCalories: 343, Total Fat: 36g, Sodium: 578mg, Carbohydrates: 4g, Protein: 24g.

Turkey Croquettes

Servings: 10
Cooking Time: 20 Minutes
Ingredients:

- Nonstick cooking spray
- 2 ½ cups turkey, cooked
- 1 stalk celery, chopped
- 2 green onions, chopped
- ½ cup cauliflower, cooked
- ½ cup broccoli, cooked
- 1 cup stuffing, cooked
- 1 cup cracker crumbs
- 1 egg, lightly beaten
- 1/8 tsp salt
- 1/8 tsp pepper
- 1 cup French fried onions, crushed

Directions:
1. Spray the fryer basket with cooking spray.
2. Add the turkey, celery, onion, cauliflower, and broccoli to a food processor and pulse until finely chopped. Transfer to a large bowl.
3. Stir in stuffing and 1 cup of the cracker crumbs until combined.
4. Add the egg, salt and pepper and stir to combine. Form into 10 patties.
5. Place the crushed fried onions in a shallow dish. Coat patties on both sides in the onions and place in the basket. Lightly spray the tops with cooking spray.
6. Add the tender-crisp lid and set to air fry on 375°F. Cook 5-7 minutes until golden brown. Flip over and spray with cooking spray again, cook another 5-7 minutes. Serve immediately.

Nutrition Info:
- InfoCalories 133,Total Fat 4g,Total Carbs 16g,Protein 9g,Sodium 449mg.

Chicken Burrito Bowl

Servings:4
Cooking Time: 10 Minutes
Ingredients:

- 1 pound boneless, skinless chicken breasts, cut into 1-inch chunks
- 1 tablespoon chili powder
- 1½ teaspoons cumin
- 1 teaspoon sea salt
- 1 teaspoon freshly ground black pepper
- ½ teaspoon paprika
- ¼ teaspoon garlic powder
- ¼ teaspoon onion powder
- ¼ teaspoon cayenne pepper
- ¼ teaspoon dried oregano
- 1 cup chicken stock
- ¼ cup water
- 1¼ cups of your favorite salsa
- 1 can corn kernels, drained
- 1 can black beans, rinsed and drained
- 1 cup rice
- ¾ cup shredded Cheddar cheese

Directions:
1. Add the chicken, chili powder, cumin, salt, black pepper, paprika, garlic powder, onion powder, cayenne pepper, oregano, chicken stock, water, salsa, corn, and beans and stir well.
2. Add the rice to the top of the ingredients in the pot. Assemble pressure lid, making sure the pressure release valve is in the SEAL position.
3. Select PRESSURE and set to HI. Set time to 10 minutes. Select START/STOP to begin.
4. When pressure cooking is complete, quick release the pressure by moving the pressure release valve to the VENT position. Carefully remove lid when the unit has finished releasing pressure.
5. Add the cheese and stir. Serve immediately.

Nutrition Info:
- InfoCalories: 570,Total Fat: 11g,Sodium: 1344mg,Carbohydrates: 77g,Protein: 45g.

Chicken With Mushroom Sauce

Servings: 10
Cooking Time: 6 Hours
Ingredients:
- 8 oz. tomato sauce
- 1 cup mushrooms, sliced
- ½ cup dry white wine
- 1 onion, chopped
- 1 clove garlic, chopped fine
- ¼ tsp salt
- ¼ tsp pepper
- 3 lbs. chicken pieces, skinless
- 2 tbsp. water
- 1 tbsp. flour

Directions:
1. Add the tomato sauce, mushrooms, wine, onion, garlic, salt and pepper to the cooking pot, stir to mix.
2. Add the chicken and turn to coat well
3. Add the lid and set to slow cook on low heat. Cook 6 hours or until chicken is cooked through and tender. Transfer chicken to a serving plate.
4. In a small bowl, whisk together water and flour until smooth. Stir into the sauce and cook 10-15 minutes, stirring frequently, until sauce thickens. Serve chicken topped with sauce.

Nutrition Info:
- InfoCalories 176,Total Fat 4g,Total Carbs 4g,Protein 28g,Sodium 164mg.

Chicken And Broccoli Stir-fry

Servings:4
Cooking Time: 20 Minutes
Ingredients:
- 1 cup long-grain white rice
- 1 cup chicken stock
- 2 tablespoons canola oil
- 3 boneless, skinless chicken breasts, cut into 1-inch cubes
- 1 medium head broccoli, cut into 1-inch florets
- 2 teaspoons kosher salt
- ½ teaspoon freshly ground black pepper
- 1 tablespoon ground ginger
- ¼ cup teriyaki sauce
- Sesame seeds, for garnish

Directions:
1. Place the rice and chicken stock into the pot. Assemble pressure lid, making sure the pressure release valve is in the SEAL position.
2. Select PRESSURE and set to HI. Set time to 2 minutes. Select START/STOP to begin.
3. When pressure cooking is complete, allow pressure to naturally release for 10 minutes. After 10 minutes, quick release remaining pressure by turning the pressure release valve to the VENT position. Carefully remove lid when unit has finished releasing pressure.
4. Transfer the rice to a bowl and cover to keep warm. Clean the cooking pot and return to unit.
5. Select SEAR/SAUTÉ and set to HI. Select START/STOP to begin. Let preheat for 5 minutes.
6. Add the oil and heat for 1 minute. Add the chicken and cook, stirring frequently, for about 6 minutes.
7. Stir in the broccoli, salt, pepper, and ginger. Cook for 5 minutes, stirring frequently. Stir in the teriyaki sauce and cook, stirring frequently, until the chicken has reached internal temperature of 165°F on a food thermometer.
8. Serve the chicken and broccoli mixture over the rice. Garnish with sesame seeds if desired.

Nutrition Info:
- InfoCalories: 425,Total Fat: 10g,Sodium: 1176mg,Carbohydrates: 49g,Protein: 35g.

Chicken Chickpea Chili

Servings: 4
Cooking Time: 25 Min
Ingredients:

- 1 pound boneless; skinless chicken breast; cubed /450g
- 2 cans chickpeas, drained and rinsed /435g
- 1 jalapeño pepper; diced
- 1 lime; cut into six wedges
- 3 large serrano peppers; diced
- 1 onion; diced
- ½ cup chopped fresh cilantro /65g
- ½ cup shredded Monterey Jack cheese /65g
- 2 ½ cups water; divided /675ml
- 1 tbsp olive oil /15ml
- 2 tbsp chili powder /30g
- 1 tsp ground cumin /5g
- 1 tsp minced fresh garlic /5g
- 1 tsp salt /5g

Directions:
1. Warm oil on Sear/Sauté. Add in onion, serrano peppers, and jalapeno pepper and cook for 5 minutes until tender; add salt, cumin and garlic for seasoning.
2. Stir chicken with vegetable mixture; cook for 3 to 6 minutes until no longer pink; add 2 cups or 500ml water and chickpeas.
3. Seal the pressure lid, choose Pressure, set to High, and set the timer to 5 minutes. Press Start. Release pressure naturally for 5 minutes. Press Start. Stir chili powder with remaining ½ cup or 125ml water; mix in chili.
4. Press Sear/Sauté. Boil the chili as you stir and cook until slightly thickened. Divide chili into plates; garnish with cheese and cilantro. Over the chili, squeeze a lime wedge.

Turkey & Squash Casserole

Servings: 8
Cooking Time: 55 Minutes
Ingredients:

- 2 tsp olive oil
- 1 onion, chopped
- 1 lb. zucchini, sliced ¼-inch thick
- 1 lb. yellow squash, sliced ¼-inch thick
- 14 ½ oz. tomatoes, diced
- ¼ cup fresh basil, chopped
- 1 tsp garlic powder
- 10 ¾ oz. cream of chicken soup, low sodium
- 1 cup sour cream, fat free
- 1 cup sharp cheddar cheese, reduced fat, grated
- 4 cups turkey, cooked & chopped
- ½ tsp black pepper
- 2 tbsp. whole wheat bread crumbs

Directions:
1. Add the oil to the cooking pot and set to sauté on med-high heat.
2. Add the onion, zucchini, and yellow squash and cook until soft, about 10 minutes.
3. Transfer to a large bowl and stir in tomatoes, basil, and garlic powder.
4. In a medium bowl, combine soup, sour cream, cheese, turkey, and pepper, mix well.
5. Spread half the vegetable mixture on the bottom of the pot. Top with half the chicken mixture. Repeat. Sprinkle the bread crumbs over the top.
6. Add the tender-crisp lid and set to bake on 350°F. Bake 45 minutes or until hot and bubbly. Serve.

Nutrition Info:
- InfoCalories 219,Total Fat 5g,Total Carbs 18g,Protein 25g,Sodium 469mg.

Turkey Green Chili

Servings: 8
Cooking Time: 4 Hours
Ingredients:
- Nonstick cooking spray
- 2 poblano chilies
- 1 ½ lbs. fresh green tomatillos
- 5 cloves garlic, peel on
- 3 cloves garlic, chopped fine
- 1 jalapeno, seeded & chopped
- 1 bunch of cilantro, chopped
- 2 tsp salt, divided
- 2 tbsp. lime juice
- 1/8 tsp sugar
-
- 3 lbs. turkey thighs
- 2 tbsp. extra virgin olive oil
- 3 cups onion, chopped
- 1 teaspoon cumin
- 2 ½ cups chicken broth, low sodium
- 1 tsp chipotle powder
- 2 tbsp. fresh oregano, chopped
- 2 bay leaves
- 1/8 tsp ground cloves

Directions:
1. Lightly spray the fryer basket with cooking spray.
2. Place the poblano's in the basket. Add the tender-crisp lid and set to broil. Cook chilies until they have charred on all sides, turning every couple of minutes. Transfer to a paper bag, close and let the chilies sit for 5 minutes.
3. After 5 minutes, remove the charred skin, stems and seeds from the chilies.
4. Place the tomatillos, cut side down, in the fryer basket along with the garlic cloves. Add the tender-crisp lid and broil 5-7 minutes until nicely browned. Let cool to the touch then remove the garlic peel.
5. Place the tomatillos, garlic, jalapeno, poblanos, cilantro, 1 teaspoon salt, lime juice, and sugar in a blender. Process on low to start, then increase the speed until mixture is smooth.
6. Season the turkey with salt and pepper.
7. Add the oil to the cooking pot and set to sear on med-high. Add the turkey, in batches, and sear until lightly browned on all sides. Transfer to a plate.
8. Add the onions and cumin and cook, stirring to scrape up any brown bits on the bottom of the pot, until onions are translucent. Add the chopped garlic and cook 30 seconds more.
9. Add the tomatillo sauce, broth, chipotle powder, oregano, bay leaves, 1 teaspoon salt, ½ teaspoon pepper, and clove to the pot and stir to mix. Add the turkey and turn to coat well.
10. Add the lid and set to slow cook on high. Cook 3-4 hours or until turkey starts to fall off the bone. Transfer turkey to a work surface and remove the skin and bones. Chop the meat and return it to the pot. Serve, this is delicious on its own or makes a great filling for burritos.

Nutrition Info:
- InfoCalories 97,Total Fat 5g,Total Carbs 3g,Protein 9g,Sodium 337mg.

Bacon Lime Chicken

Servings: 4
Cooking Time: 30 Minutes
Ingredients:
- 8 chicken thighs, boneless & skinless
- 1 tsp salt
- 2 tsp honey
- 1 tsp granulated garlic
- 1 tsp granulated onion
-
- ½ tsp pepper
- 2 tsp lime juice
- ¼ tsp cayenne pepper
- 8 slices bacon

Directions:
1. Place the chicken and seasonings in a large bowl. Use your hands to mix and rub the seasonings into the meat until chicken is evenly coated.
2. Roll the chicken along the long side and wrap each with a slice of bacon.
3. Place chicken in the fryer basket, with bacon ends on the bottom. Add the tender-crisp lid and set to air fry on 400°F. Cook chicken 25-30 minutes, turning over halfway through cooking time. Serve hot.

Nutrition Info:
- InfoCalories 371,Total Fat 23g,Total Carbs 6g,Protein 32g,Sodium 878mg.

Chicken Pasta With Pesto Sauce

Servings: 8
Cooking Time: 30 Min

Ingredients:
- 4 chicken breast, boneless, skinless; cubed
- 8 oz. macaroni pasta /240g
- 1 garlic clove; minced
- 1/4 cup Asiago cheese, grated /32.5g
- 2 cups fresh collard greens, trimmed /260g
- ¼ cup cream cheese, at room temperature /32.5g
- 1 cup cherry tomatoes, halved /130g
- ½ cup basil pesto sauce /125ml
- 3½ cups water /875ml
- 1 tbsp butter /15g
- 1 tbsp salt; divided/15g
- 1 tsp freshly ground black pepper to taste /5g
- Freshly chopped basil for garnish

Directions:
1. To the inner steel pot of the Foodi, add water, chicken, 2 tsp salt, butter, and macaroni, and stir well to mix and be submerged in water.
2. Seal the pressure lid, choose Pressure, set to High, and set the timer to 2 minutes. Press Start. When ready, release the pressure quickly. Press Start/Stop, open the lid, get rid of ¼ cup water from the pot.
3. Set on Sear/Sauté. Into the pot, mix in collard greens, pesto sauce, garlic, remaining 1 tsp o 5g salt, cream cheese, tomatoes, and black pepper. Cook, for 1 to 2 minutes as you stir, until sauce is creamy.
4. Place the pasta into serving plates; top with asiago cheese and basil before serving.

Chicken Piccata

Servings: 4
Cooking Time: 4 Hours

Ingredients:
- Nonstick cooking spray
- ¼ cup flour
- 1 tsp garlic powder
- ½ tsp salt
- ¼ tsp pepper
- 2 chicken breasts, boneless, skinless & halved horizontally
- 2 cups chicken broth, low sodium
- 1 tbsp. fresh lemon juice
- ½ cup heavy cream

Directions:
1. Spray the cooking pot with cooking spray.
2. In a small bowl, combine flour, garlic powder, salt, and pepper, mix well.
3. Coat chicken in flour mixture on all sides. Set the cooker to sear and add the chicken, brown on both sides. Pour in broth.
4. Add the lid and set to slow cook on low. Cook 4 hours or until chicken is cooked through.
5. Stir in lemon juice and cream. Season with salt and pepper and increase temperature to high. Cook another 10 minutes until sauce has thickened slightly.
6. Transfer chicken to serving plates and top with sauce. Serve.

Nutrition Info:
- InfoCalories 248,Total Fat 10g,Total Carbs 8g,Protein 31g,Sodium 1071mg.

Mini Turkey Loaves

Servings: 6
Cooking Time: 35 Minutes
Ingredients:
- 6 tbsp. barbecue sauce, divided
- 2 tbsp. water
- 2/3 cup oats
- 2 egg whites, lightly beaten
- 2 tsp chili powder
- 2 tsp Worcestershire sauce
- ½ tsp salt
- 1 lb. ground turkey
- 1 onion, chopped fine
- ½ green bell pepper, chopped fine

Directions:
1. Place the rack in the cooking pot and top with a sheet of foil.
2. In a large bowl, combine 3 tablespoons barbecue sauce and water, stir to mix well.
3. Stir in the oats, egg whites, chili powder, Worcestershire, and salt and mix well.
4. Add the turkey, onion, and bell pepper and mix to combine. Form into 6 small oval-shaped loaves and place on the foil.
5. Add the tender-crisp lid and set to bake on 375°F. Bake 30 minutes.
6. Open the lid and spread the remaining barbecue sauce over the tops of the meatloaves. Bake another 5 minutes. Serve.

Nutrition Info:
- InfoCalories 250,Total Fat 11g,Total Carbs 21g,Protein 17g,Sodium 448mg.

Chicken Stroganoff With Fetucini

Servings: 4
Cooking Time: 35 Min
Ingredients:
- 2 large boneless skinless chicken breasts
- 8 ounces fettucini /240g
- ½ cup sliced onion /65g
- ½ cup dry white wine /125ml
- 1 cup sautéed mushrooms /130g
- ¼ cup heavy cream /62.5ml
- 1 ½ cups water /375ml
- 2 cups chicken stock /500ml
- 2 tbsp butter /30g
- 1 tbsp flour /15g
- 2 tbsp chopped fresh dill to garnish /30g
- ½ tsp Worcestershire sauce /2.5ml
- 1½ tsp salt /7.5g

Directions:
1. Season the chicken on both sides with salt and set aside. Choose Sear/Sauté and adjust to Medium. Press Start to preheat the pot. Melt the butter and sauté the onion until brown, about 3 minutes.
2. Mix in the flour to make a roux, about 2 minutes and gradually pour in the dry white wine while stirring and scraping the bottom of the pot to release any browned bits. Allow the white wine to simmer and to reduce by two-thirds.
3. Pour in the water, chicken stock, 1 tbsp or 15g of salt, and fettucini. Mix and arrange the chicken on top of the fettucini.
4. Lock the pressure lid to Seal. Choose Pressure; adjust the pressure to High and the cook time to 5 minutes; press Start. When done pressure-cooking, perform a quick pressure release.
5. Transfer the chicken breasts to a cutting board to cool slightly, and then cut into bite-size chunks. Return the chicken to the pot and stir in the Worcestershire sauce and mushrooms. Add the heavy cream and cook until the mixture stops simmering. Ladle the stroganoff into bowls and garnish with dill.

Hainanese Chicken

Servings: 4
Cooking Time: 4 Hours

Ingredients:

- 1 ounce's ginger, peeled
- 6 garlic cloves, crushed
- 6 bundles cilantro/basil leaves
- 1 teaspoon salt
- 1 tablespoon sesame oil
- 3 1 and ½ pounds each chicken meat, ready to cook
- For Dip
-
- 2 tablespoons ginger, minced
- 1 teaspoon garlic, minced
- 1 tablespoon chicken stock
- 1 teaspoon sesame oil
- ½ teaspoon erythritol
- Salt to taste

Directions:

1. Add chicken, garlic, ginger, leaves, and salt to your Ninja Food.
2. Add enough water to fully submerge chicken; Lock and secure the Ninja Foodi's lid cooks on SLOW COOK mode on LOW for 4 hours.
3. Release pressure naturally.
4. Take chicken out of the pot and chill for 10 minutes.
5. Take a suitable and add all the dipping ingredients and blend well in a food processor.
6. Take chicken out of ice bath and drain, chop into serving pieces.
7. Set onto a serving platter.
8. Brush chicken with sesame oil.
9. Serve with ginger dip.
10. Enjoy.

Nutrition Info:

- InfoCalories: 535; Fat: 45g; Carbohydrates: 5g; Protein: 28g

Herby Chicken With Asparagus Sauce

Servings: 4
Cooking Time: 1 Hr

Ingredients:

- 1 Young Whole Chicken /1575g
- 8 ounces asparagus, trimmed and chopped /240g
- 1 onion; chopped
- 1 cup chicken stock /250ml
- 4 fresh thyme; minced
- 3 fresh rosemary; minced
- 4 garlic cloves; minced
- 2 lemons, zested and quartered
-
- 1 fresh thyme sprig
- 1 tbsp flour /15g
- 1 tbsp soy sauce /15ml
- 2 tbsp olive oil /30ml
- 1 tsp olive oil /5ml
- Cooking spray
- salt and freshly ground black pepper to taste
- Chopped parsley to garnish

Directions:

1. Rub all sides of the chicken with garlic, rosemary, black pepper, lemon zest; minced thyme, and salt. Into the chicken cavity, insert lemon wedges.
2. Warm oil on Sear/Sauté. Add in onion and asparagus, and cook for 5 minutes until softened. Mix in chicken stock, 1 thyme sprig, black pepper, soy sauce, and salt.
3. Into the inner pot, set trivet over asparagus mixture. On top of the trivet, place your chicken with breast-side up.
4. Seal the pressure lid, choose Pressure, set to High, and set the timer to 20 minutes. Press Start. Once ready, do a quick release. Remove the chicken to a serving platter.
5. In the inner pot, sprinkle flour over asparagus mixture and blend the sauce with an immersion blender until desired consistency. Top the chicken with asparagus sauce and garnish with parsley.

Caprese Stuffed Chicken

Servings: 4
Cooking Time: 15 Minutes
Ingredients:
- Nonstick cooking spray
- 4 chicken breasts boneless & skinless
- 2 Roma tomatoes, sliced ¼-inch thick
- ¾ cup mozzarella cheese, grated
- 1 tsp salt
- ½ tsp pepper
- ¼ cup fresh basil, chopped
- 2 tbsp. dark balsamic vinegar

Directions:
1. Spray the cooking pot with cooking spray.
2. Cut the chicken horizontally to create a pocket, being careful not to cut all the way through.
3. Stuff the pockets with tomatoes and cheese, secure with a toothpick. Season the chicken with salt and pepper.
4. Set cooker to sauté on medium heat. Add the chicken and sear on one side until light brown, about 5 minutes. Carefully turn the chicken over.
5. Add the tender-crisp lid and to bake on 400°F. cook chicken about 10 minutes or until cooked through.
6. Transfer to serving plates and top with basil and a drizzle of the balsamic vinegar. Serve.

Nutrition Info:
- InfoCalories 258,Total Fat 6g,Total Carbs 3g,Protein 30g,Sodium 847mg.

Chicken With Bacon And Beans

Servings: 4
Cooking Time: 45 Min
Ingredients:
- 4 boneless; skinless chicken thighs
- 4 garlic cloves; minced
- 15 ounces red kidney beans, drained and rinsed /450g
- 4 slices bacon, crumbled
- 1 can whole tomatoes /435g
- 1 red bell pepper; chopped
- 1 onion; diced
- 1 cup shredded Monterey Jack cheese /130g
- 1 cup sliced red onion /130g
- ¼ cup chopped cilantro /32.5g
-
- 1 cup chicken broth /250ml
- 1 tbsp tomato paste /15ml
- 1 tbsp olive oil /15ml
- 1 tbsp oregano /15g
- 1 tbsp ground cumin/15g
- 1 tsp chili powder /5g
- ½ tsp cayenne pepper /2.5g
- 1 tsp salt /5g
- 1 cup cooked corn /130g

Directions:
1. Warm oil on Sear/Sauté. Sear the chicken for 3 minutes for each side until browned. Set the chicken on a plate. In the same oil, fry bacon until crispy, about 5 minutes and set aside.
2. Add in onions and cook for 2 to 3 minutes until fragrant. Stir in garlic, oregano, cayenne pepper, cumin, tomato paste, bell pepper, and chili powder and cook for 30 more seconds. Pour the chicken broth, salt, and tomatoes and bring to a boil. Press Start/Stop.
3. Take back the chicken and bacon to the pot and ensure it is submerged in the braising liquid. Seal the pressure lid, choose Pressure, set to High, and set the timer to 15 minutes. Press Start. When ready, release the pressure quickly.
4. Pour the kidney beans in the cooker, press Sear/Sauté and bring the liquid to a boil; cook for 10 minutes. Serve topped with shredded cheese and chopped cilantro.

Indian Butter Chicken

Servings: 8
Cooking Time: 15 Minutes

Ingredients:
- 2 14 oz. cans tomatoes, diced & undrained
- 2 jalapeño peppers, seeded & chopped
- 2 tbsp. fresh ginger, peeled & chopped
- 1 tbsp. paprika
- 2 tsp cumin
- 2 tsp garam masala
- 2 tsp salt
- ½ cup butter, unsalted
- 10 chicken thighs, boneless & skinless
- 2 tbsp. cornstarch
- 2 tbsp. water
- ¾ cup heavy cream
- ¾ cup plain Greek yogurt
- ¼ cup cilantro, chopped & packed

Directions:
1. Add the tomatoes, jalapenos, ginger, paprika, cumin, garam masala, and salt to a food processor or blender, pulse until pureed.
2. Add the butter to the cooking pot and set to sauté on medium heat.
3. Once butter has melted, add chicken, a few at a time, and cook until nicely browned on all sides. Transfer chicken to a cutting board.
4. Add tomato mixture and cook, stirring up all the brown bits on the bottom of the pot. Turn off the heat.
5. Slice the chicken into bite-size pieces and return to the pot with the cooking juices, stir to mix.
6. Add the lid and set to pressure cook on high. Set the timer for 5 minutes. Once the timer goes off use quick release to remove the pressure.
7. In a small bowl, whisk together cornstarch and water until smooth. Add to the cooking pot and set to sauté on med-high heat. Bring to a boil and cook until sauce has thickened, about 1-2 minutes.
8. Turn off the heat and stir in sour cream, yogurt, and cilantro. Serve.

Nutrition Info:
- InfoCalories 376,Total Fat 26g,Total Carbs 8g,Protein 27g,Sodium 1296mg.

Spicy Chicken Wings.

Servings: 2
Cooking Time: 25 Min

Ingredients:
- 10 chicken wings
- ½ tbsp honey /15ml
- 2 tbsp hot chili sauce /30ml
- ½ tbsp lime juice /7.5ml
- ½ tsp kosher salt /2.5g
- ½ tsp black pepper /2.5g

Directions:
1. Mix the lime juice, honey, and chili sauce. Toss the mixture over the chicken wings.
2. Put the wings in the fryer's basket, close the crisping lid and cook for 25 minutes on Air Crisp mode at 350 °F or 177°C. Shake the basket every 5 minutes.

Chicken With Cilantro Rice

Servings: 4
Cooking Time: 70 Min
Ingredients:
- 1 pound bone-in, skin-on chicken thighs /450g
- 1 cup basmati rice /130g
- ¾ cup chicken broth /188ml
- ½ cup tomato sauce /125ml
- 1 red onion; diced
- 1 yellow bell pepper; diced
- 2 tbsp ghee divided /30g
- 1 tbsp cayenne powder /15g
- 1 tsp ground cumin /5g
- 1 tsp Italian herb mix /5g
- ½ tsp salt /2.5g
- Chopped fresh cilantro, for garnish
- Lime wedges; for serving

Directions:
1. Choose Sear/Sauté on the pot and set to Medium High. Choose Start/Stop to preheat the pot. Melt half of the ghee in the pot, and cook the onion for 3 minutes, stirring occasionally, until softened.
2. Include the yellow bell pepper, cayenne pepper, cumin, herb mix, and salt, and cook for 2 minutes more with frequent stirring.
3. Pour the rice, broth, and tomato sauce into the pot. Place the reversible rack in the higher position of the pot, which is over the rice. Put the chicken on the rack.
4. Seal the pressure lid, choose pressure, set to High, and set the time to 30 minutes. Choose Start/Stop to begin cooking the rice. When the time is over, perform a quick pressure release and carefully open the lid.
5. Brush the chicken thighs with the remaining 1 tbsp or 15g of ghee. Close the crisping lid. Choose Broil and set the time to 5 minutes. Press Start/Stop.
6. When ready, check for your desired crispiness and remove the rack from the pot. Plate the chicken, garnish with cilantro, and serve with lime wedges.

Italian Turkey & Pasta Soup

Servings: 8
Cooking Time: 10 Minutes
Ingredients:
- 1 lb. ground turkey sausage
- 1 onion, chopped fine
- 5 cloves garlic, chopped fine
- 1 green bell pepper, chopped fine
- 1 tbsp. Italian seasoning
- 2 15 oz. cans tomatoes, diced
- 2 8 oz. cans tomato sauce
- 4 cups chicken broth, low sodium
- 3 cups whole wheat pasta
- ¼ cup parmesan cheese
- ¼ cup mozzarella cheese, grated

Directions:
1. Add the sausage, onions, and garlic to the cooking pot. Set to sauté on med-high and cook, breaking sausage up, until meat is no longer pink and onions are translucent. Drain off excess fat.
2. Stir in bell pepper, Italian seasoning, tomatoes, tomato sauce, broth, and pasta, mix well.
3. Add the lid and set to pressure cook on high. Set the timer for 5 minutes. Once the timer goes off, use the natural release for 5-10 minutes, then quick release to remove the pressure.
4. Stir the soup and ladle into bowls. Serve garnished with parmesan and mozzarella cheeses.

Nutrition Info:
- InfoCalories 294,Total Fat 8g,Total Carbs 37g,Protein 22g,Sodium 841mg.

Riviera Chicken

Servings: 4
Cooking Time: 20 Minutes

Ingredients:
- Nonstick cooking spray
- 4 chicken breast halves, boneless & skinless
- 1/8 tsp salt
- 1/8 tsp pepper
- 14 ½ oz. tomatoes with basil, garlic, and oregano, diced
- ½ cup black olives, sliced
- 1 tbsp. lemon zest, grated fine
- 2 cloves garlic, chopped fine

Directions:
1. Spray the cooking pot with cooking spray and set to sauté on med-high heat.
2. Season chicken with salt and pepper and add to the pot. Cook 5-7 minutes per side, until no longer pink. Transfer chicken to a plate and reduce heat to medium.
3. Add remaining ingredients to the pot and cook 4 minutes or until hot, stirring occasionally. Return the chicken to the pot and cook until heated through. Serve immediately.

Nutrition Info:
- InfoCalories 175,Total Fat 5g,Total Carbs 5g,Protein 27g,Sodium 371mg.

Blackened Turkey Cutlets

Servings: 4
Cooking Time: 5 Minutes

Ingredients:
- Nonstick cooking spray
- 2 tsp paprika
- 1 tsp thyme
- ½ tsp sugar
- ½ tsp onion powder
- ½ tsp garlic powder
- ½ tsp salt
- ½ tsp pepper
- ¼ tsp cayenne pepper
- 4 turkey breast cutlets, boneless & skinless

Directions:
1. Spray the fryer basket with cooking spray.
2. In a small bowl, combine everything but the turkey and mix well. Rub both sides of the cutlets with the seasoning mixture and place in the basket.
3. Add the tender-crisp lid and set to air fry on 350°F. Cook 4-5 minutes per side or until turkey is cooked through. Serve immediately.

Nutrition Info:
- InfoCalories 134,Total Fat 2g,Total Carbs 1g,Protein 27g,Sodium 419mg.

Turkey & Cabbage Enchiladas

Servings: 4
Cooking Time: 30 Minutes

Ingredients:
- Nonstick cooking spray
- 8 large cabbage leaves
- 1 tbsp. olive oil
- ½ cup onion, chopped
- ½ red bell pepper, chopped
- 3 cloves garlic, chopped fine
- 2 tsp cumin
- 1 tbsp. chili powder
- 1 tsp salt
- ¼ tsp crushed red pepper flakes
- 2 cups turkey, cooked & shredded
- 1 cup enchilada sauce, sugar free
- ½ cup cheddar cheese, fat free, grated

Directions:
1. Spray a small baking dish with cooking spray.
2. Bring a large pot of water to boil. Add cabbage leaves and cook 30 seconds. Transfer leaves to paper towel lined surface and pat dry.
3. Add the oil to the cooking pot and set to sauté on medium heat.
4. Add the onion, bell pepper, and garlic and cook, stirring occasionally, until onions are translucent, about 5 minutes.
5. Stir in cumin, chili powder, salt, red pepper flakes, and turkey. Cook just until heat through. Transfer mixture to a bowl.
6. Add the rack to the cooking pot.
7. Lay cabbage leaves on work surface. Divide turkey mixture evenly between leaves. Fold in the sides and roll up. Place in the prepared dish, seam side down. Pour the enchilada sauce over the top and sprinkle with cheese.
8. Place dish on the rack and add the tender-crisp lid. Set to bake on 400°F. Cook enchiladas 15-20 minutes until cheese is melted and bubbly. Let rest 5 minutes before serving.

Nutrition Info:
- InfoCalories 289,Total Fat 12g,Total Carbs 4g,Protein 32g,Sodium 735mg.

Beef, Pork & Lamb

Pot Roast With Biscuits

Servings: 6
Cooking Time: 75 Min
Ingredients:
- 1 chuck roast /1350g
- 1 pound small butternut squash; diced /450g
- 1 small red onion, peeled and quartered
- 2 carrots, peeled and cut into 1-inch pieces
- 6 refrigerated biscuits
- 1 bay leaf
- ⅔ cup dry red wine /176ml
- ⅔ cup beef broth /176ml
- ¾ cup frozen pearl onions /98g
- 2 tbsp olive oil /30ml
- 1½ tsp salt /7.5g
- 1 tsp dried oregano leaves /5g
- ¼ tsp black pepper /1.25g

Directions:
1. On the Foodi, choose Sear/Sauté and adjust to Medium-High. Press Start to preheat the pot. Heat the olive oil until shimmering. Season the beef on both sides with salt and add to the pot. Cook, undisturbed, for 3 minutes or until deeply browned. Flip the roast over and brown the other side for 3 minutes. Transfer the beef to a wire rack.
2. Pour the oil out of the pot and add the wine to the pot. Stir with a wooden spoon, scraping the bottom of the pot to let off any browned bits. Bring to a boil and cook for 1 to 2 minutes or until the wine has reduced by half.
3. Mix in the beef broth, oregano, bay leaf, black pepper, and red onion. Stir to combine and add the beef with its juices. Seal the pressure lid and choose Pressure; adjust the pressure to High and the cook time to 35 minutes. Press Start to begin cooking.
4. After cooking, perform a quick pressure release. Carefully open the pressure lid.
5. Add the butternut squash, carrots, and pearl onions to the pot. Lock the pressure lid into place, set to Seal position and Choose Pressure; adjust the pressure to High and the cook time to 2 minutes. Press Start to cook the vegetables.
6. After cooking, perform a quick pressure release, and open the lid. Transfer the beef to a cutting board and cover with aluminum foil.
7. Put the reversible rack in the upper position of the pot and cover with a circular piece of aluminum foil. Put the biscuits on the rack and put the rack in the pot.
8. Close the crisping lid and Choose Bake/Roast; adjust the temperature to 300°F and the cook time to 15 minutes. Press Start. After 8 minutes, open the lid and carefully flip the biscuits over. After baking, remove the rack and biscuits. Allow the biscuits to cool for a few minutes before serving.
9. While the biscuits cook, remove the foil from the beef and cut it against the grain into slices. Remove and discard the bay leaf and transfer the beef to a serving platter. Spoon the vegetables and the sauce over the beef. Serve with the biscuits.

Barbecue Pork Ribs

Servings: 2
Cooking Time: 4 H 35 Min
Ingredients:
- 1 lb. pork ribs /450g
- 3 garlic cloves; chopped
- 1 tbsp honey, plus more for brushing /15ml
- 4 tbsp barbecue sauce /60ml
- 1 tsp black pepper /5g
- 1 tsp sesame oil /5ml
- ½ tsp five spice powder /2.5g
- 1 tsp salt /5g
- 1 tsp soy sauce /5ml

Directions:
1. Chop the ribs into smaller pieces and place in a large bowl. In a separate bowl, whisk together all of the other ingredients. Add to the bowl with the pork, and mix until the pork is thoroughly coated. Cover the bowl, place it in the fridge, and let it marinade for about 4 hours.
2. Place the ribs in the basket of the Foodi. Close the crisping lid and cook for 15 minutes on Air Crisp mode at 350 °F or 177°C. After, brush the ribs with some honey and cook for 15 more minutes.

Greek Beef Gyros

Servings: 4
Cooking Time: 55 Min
Ingredients:
- 1 pound beef sirloin; cut into thin strips /450g
- 1 onion, thinly sliced
- 4 slices pita bread
- 1 clove garlic; minced
- 1 cup Greek yogurt /130g
- ⅓ cup beef broth /88ml
- 2 tbsp fresh dill; chopped /30g
- 2 tbsp fresh lemon juice /30ml
- 2 tbsp olive oil /30ml
- 2 tsp dry oregano /10g
- salt and ground black pepper to taste

Directions:
1. In the Foodi, mix beef, beef broth, oregano, garlic, lemon juice, pepper, onion, olive oil, and salt.
2. Seal the pressure lid, choose Pressure, set to High, and set the timer to 30 minutes. Press Start. Release pressure naturally for 15 minutes, then turn steam vent valve to Venting to release the remaining pressure quickly. Divide the beef mixture between the pita bread slices, top with yogurt and dill, and roll up to serve.

Char Siew Pork Ribs

Servings: 6
Cooking Time: 4 Hours 55 Min
Ingredients:
- 2 lb. pork ribs /900g
- 2 tbsp char siew sauce /30ml
- 2 tbsp minced ginger /30g
- 2 tbsp hoisin sauce /30ml
- 2 tbsp sesame oil /30ml
- 1 tbsp honey /15ml
- 4 garlic cloves; minced
- 1 tbsp soy sauce /15ml

Directions:
1. Whisk together all marinade ingredients, in a small bowl. Coat the ribs well with the mixture. Place in a container with a lid, and refrigerate for 4 hours.
2. Place the ribs in the basket but do not throw away the liquid from the container. Close the crisping lid and cook for 40 minutes on Air Crisp at 350 °F or 177°C. Stir in the liquid, increase the temperature to 350 °F or 177°C, and cook for 10 minutes.

Korean Cabbage Cups

Servings: 4
Cooking Time: 15 Minutes
Ingredients:
- 1 lb. lean ground beef
- 1 onion, chopped
- 4 cloves garlic, chopped fine
- 2 tsp fresh ginger, grated
- 1 tbsp. sesame oil
- 3 tbsp. soy sauce, low sodium
- 1 tsp red chili paste
- 2 tbsp. rice wine vinegar
- 8 large cabbage leaves
- ¼ cup green onion, chopped
- ¼ cup cilantro, chopped

Directions:
1. Add the beef to the cooking pot and set to sauté on med-high heat. Cook, breaking up with a spatula, until no longer pink, about 5 minutes. Drain off fat.
2. Add onion, garlic, ginger, and sesame oil and cook until onion becomes translucent, about 3-5 minutes.
3. Stir in the soy sauce, chili paste, and vinegar and bring to a simmer. Simmer, stirring occasionally, about 3 minutes.
4. Lay the cabbage leaves on serving plates, two to a plate. Spoon 2-3 tablespoons of beef mixture on each leaf and top with green onion and cilantro. Serve hot.

Nutrition Info:
- InfoCalories 268,Total Fat 15g,Total Carbs 8g,Protein 25g,Sodium 473mg.

Mongolian Beef

Servings: 2
Cooking Time: 11 Minutes
Ingredients:
- 1 lb. flank steak, sliced
- 1/4 cup corn starch
- Sauce:
- 2 teaspoon vegetable oil
- 1/2 teaspoon ginger, minced
- 1 tablespoon garlic, minced
- 1/2 cup soy sauce
- 1/2 cup water
- 3/4 cup brown erythritol

Directions:
1. Coat the beef with corn starch. Put in the Ninja Foodi basket.
2. Seal the crisping lid. Set it to air crisp.
3. Cook at 390 °F for about 10 minutes per side.
4. Remove and set aside. Set the pot to sauté. Stir in the vegetable oil.
5. Sauté the ginger and garlic for 1 minute. Stir in the soy sauce, water and brown erythritol.
6. Pour the prepared sauce on top of the beef.

Nutrition Info:
- InfoCalories: 399; Fat: 11.7g; Carbohydrate: 39g; Protein: 33.7g

Cheesy Ham & Potato Casserole

Servings: 6
Cooking Time: 35 Minutes
Ingredients:
- 1 tbsp. butter
- 1 sweet potato, peeled & chopped
- 1 cup onion, chopped
- 2 cloves garlic, chopped fine
- 8 oz. cream cheese, low fat
- 14 ½ oz. chicken broth, low sodium
- ½ cup sour cream, low fat
- ½ tsp thyme, crushed
- ¼ tsp pepper
- 32 oz. hash brown potatoes, thawed
- 1 ½ cups white cheddar cheese, low fat, grated
- 1 cup ham, chopped
- 1 cup grape tomatoes, sliced
- 2 green onions, sliced

Directions:
1. Add butter to the cooking pot and set to sauté on medium heat. Once the butter has melted, add sweet potato, onion, and garlic and cook 5-8 minutes or until potato is tender.
2. Stir in cream cheese until melted. Add broth, sour cream, thyme, and pepper and mix well.
3. Add hash browns, cheese, and ham and mix until combined. Lay the sliced tomatoes evenly over the top.
4. Add the tender-crisp lid and set to bake on 375°F. Bake 30-35 minutes until hot and bubbly and top is lightly browned. Let rest 5 minutes, then serve garnished with green onions.

Nutrition Info:
- InfoCalories 369, Total Fat 13g, Total Carbs 41g, Protein 21g, Sodium 1541mg.

Butter Pork Chops

Servings: 4
Cooking Time: 10 Minutes
Ingredients:
- 4 pork chops
- Black pepper and salt, to taste
- 2 tablespoons butter
- 2 teaspoons garlic, minced
- 1/2 cup herbed chicken stock
- 1/2 cup heavy whip cream
- 1/2 a lemon, juiced

Directions:
1. Season the four pork chops with black pepper and salt.
2. Select "Sauté" mode on Ninja Foodi and add oil to heat up.
3. Add pork chops and sauté both sides until the golden, total for 6 minutes.
4. Remove thighs to a platter and keep it on the side.
5. Add garlic and cook for 2 minutes.
6. Whisk in chicken stock, heavy cream, lemon juice and bring the sauce to simmer and reintroduce the pork chops.
7. Lock and secure the Ninja Foodi's lid and cook for 10 minutes on "HIGH" pressure.
8. Release pressure naturally over 10 minutes.
9. Serve warm and enjoy.

Nutrition Info:
- InfoCalories: 294; Fat: 26g; Carbohydrates: 4g; Protein: 12g

Honey Short Ribs With Rosemary Potatoes

Servings: 4
Cooking Time: 105 Min
Ingredients:
- 4 bone-in beef short ribs, silver skin
- 2 potatoes, peeled and cut into 1-inch pieces
- ½ cup beef broth /125ml
- 3 garlic cloves; minced
- 1 onion; chopped
- 2 tbsp olive oil /30ml
- 2 tbsp honey /30ml
- 2 tbsp minced fresh rosemary /30ml
- 1 tsp salt /5g
- 1 tsp black pepper /5g

Directions:
1. Choose Sear/Sauté on the pot and set to High. Choose Start/Stop to preheat the pot. Season the short ribs on all sides with ½ tsp or 2.5g of salt and ½ tsp or 2.5g of pepper. Heat 1 tbsp of olive oil and brown the ribs on all sides, about 10 minutes total. Stir in the onion, honey, broth, 1 tbsp of rosemary, and garlic.
2. Seal the pressure lid, choose Pressure, set to High, and set the time to 40 minutes. Choose Start/Stop to begin. In a large bowl, toss the potatoes with the remaining oil, rosemary, salt, and black pepper.
3. When the ribs are ready, perform a quick pressure release and carefully open the lid.
4. Fix the reversible rack in the higher position of the pot, which is over the ribs. Put the potatoes on the rack. Close the crisping lid. Choose Bake/Roast, set the temperature to 350°F or 177°C, and set the time to 15 minutes. Choose Start/Stop to begin roasting.
5. Once the potatoes are tender and roasted, use tongs to pick the potatoes and the short ribs into a plate; set aside. Choose Sear/Sauté and set to High. Simmer the sauce for 5 minutes and spoon the sauce into a bowl.
6. Allow sitting for 2 minutes and scoop off the fat that forms on top. Serve the ribs with the potatoes and sauce.

Bacon & Sauerkraut With Apples

Servings: 6
Cooking Time: 30 Minutes
Ingredients:
- ¼ lb. apple-wood smoked bacon
- 1 onion, chopped fine
- 2 Granny Smith apples, peeled, cored, & grated
- 2 cloves garlic, chopped fine
- 1 tsp caraway seeds, ground
- 3 cups apple juice, unsweetened
- ¼ cup white wine vinegar
- 2 lbs. refrigerated sauerkraut, drained

Directions:
1. Add the bacon to the cooking pot and set to sauté on medium heat. Cook until bacon has browned and fat is rendered. Transfer to paper towel lined plat. Drain all but 1 tablespoon of the fat.
2. Add the onions and apples to the pot and cook 6-7 minutes, until onions are translucent. Add the garlic and caraway and cook 1 minute more.
3. Stir in apple juice and vinegar, increase heat to med-high and bring to a boil. Let boil about 5 minutes until liquid is reduced to a syrup.
4. Chop the bacon and add it and the sauerkraut to the pot, stir to mix. Reduce heat to low and cook 10 minutes until heated through and sauerkraut is tender. Salt and pepper to taste and serve.

Nutrition Info:
- InfoCalories 58,Total Fat 2g,Total Carbs 9g,Protein 1g,Sodium 170mg.

Skinny Cheesesteaks

Servings: 4
Cooking Time: 10 Minutes
Ingredients:
- ½ tbsp. olive oil
- 1 lb. lean sirloin steak, sliced in very thin strips
- ½ tsp salt
- ¼ tsp pepper
- 2 tsp oregano
- 1 onion, sliced in strips
- 1 green bell pepper, sliced in strips
- 1 red bell pepper, sliced in strips
- 8 large lettuce leaves
- ½ cup provolone cheese, low fat, grated
- 2 tbsp. cilantro, chopped

Directions:
1. Add the oil to the cooking pot and set to sauté on med-high heat.
2. Season the steak with salt and pepper and add to the pot along with the oregano, onion, and bell peppers. Cook, stirring frequently, 5-10 minutes until beef is cooked and vegetables are tender.
3. Place 2 lettuce leaves on each serving plate. Spoon beef mixture onto lettuce and tops with cheese and cilantro. Serve.

Nutrition Info:
- InfoCalories 319,Total Fat 19g,Total Carbs 7g,Protein 29g,Sodium 444mg.

Ground Beef Stuffed Empanadas

Servings: 2
Cooking Time: 60 Min

Ingredients:
- ¼ pound ground beef /112.5g
- 2 small tomatoes; chopped
- 8 square gyoza wrappers
- 1 egg, beaten
- 1 garlic clove; minced
- ½ white onion; chopped
- 6 green olives, pitted and chopped
- 1 tbsp olive oil /15ml
- ¼ tsp cumin powder /1.25g
- ¼ tsp paprika /1.25g
- ⅛ tsp cinnamon powder /0.625g

Directions:
1. Choose Sear/Sauté on the pot and set to Medium High. Choose Start/Stop to preheat the pot. Put the oil, garlic, onion, and beef in the preheated pot and cook for 5 minutes, stirring occasionally, until the fragrant and the beef is no longer pink.
2. Stir in the olives, cumin, paprika, and cinnamon and cook for an additional 3 minutes. Add the tomatoes and cook for 1 more minute.
3. Spoon the beef mixture into a plate and allow cooling for a few minutes.
4. Meanwhile, put the Crisping Basket in the pot. Close the crisping lid; choose Air Crisp, set the temperature to 400°F or 205°C, and the time to 5 minutes. Press Start.
5. Lay the gyoza wrappers on a flat surface. Place 1 to 2 tbsps of the beef mixture in the middle of each wrapper. Brush the edges of the wrapper with egg and fold in half to form a triangle. Pinch the edges together to seal.
6. Place 4 empanadas in a single layer in the preheated Basket. Close the crisping lid. Choose Air Crisp, set the temperature to 400°F or 205°C, and set the time to 7 minutes. Choose Start/Stop to begin frying.
7. Once the timer is done, remove the empanadas from the basket and transfer to a plate. Repeat with the remaining empanadas.

Gingery Beef And Broccoli

Servings: 4
Cooking Time: 70 Min

Ingredients:
- 2 pounds skirt steak; cut into strips /900g
- 1 head broccoli, trimmed into florets
- 3 scallions, thinly sliced
- 4 garlic cloves; minced
- ½ cup coconut aminos /65g
- ½ cup water, plus 3 tbsp. /170ml
- ⅔ cup dark brown sugar /88g
- 1 tbsp olive oil /15ml
- 2 tbsp cornstarch /30g
- ½ tsp ginger puree /2.5ml

Directions:
1. Choose Sear/Sauté on the pot and set to Medium High; hit Start/Stop to preheat the pot. Pour the oil and beef in the preheated pot and brown the beef strips on both sides, about 5 minutes in total. Remove the beef from the pot and set aside.
2. Add the garlic to the oil and Sear/Sauté for 1 minute or until fragrant. Stir in the coconut aminos, ½ cup or 125ml of water, brown sugar, and ginger to the pot. Mix evenly and add the beef. Seal the pressure lid, choose Pressure, set to High, and set the time to 10 minutes. Choose Start/Stop to begin cooking.
3. Meanwhile, in a small bowl whisk combine the cornstarch and the remaining water.
4. When done cooking, perform a quick pressure release. Choose Sear/Sauté and set to Medium Low. Choose Start/Stop. Pour in the cornstarch mixture and stir continuously until the sauce becomes syrupy. Add the broccoli, stir to coat in the sauce, and cook for another 5 minutes. Once ready, garnish with scallions, and serve.

Crispy Roast Pork

Servings: 4
Cooking Time: 50 Min
Ingredients:
- 4 pork tenderloins
- ¾ tsp garlic powder /3.75g
- 1 tsp five spice seasoning /5g
- ½ tsp white pepper /2.5g
- 1 tsp salt /5g
- Cooking spray

Directions:
1. Place the pork, white pepper, garlic powder, five seasoning, and salt into a bowl and toss to coat. Leave to marinate at room temperature for 30 minutes.
2. Place the pork into the Foodi basket, greased with cooking spray, close the crisping lid and cook for 20 minutes at 360 °F or 183°C. After 10 minutes, turn the tenderloins. Serve hot.

Southern Sweet Ham

Servings: 12
Cooking Time: 8 Hours
Ingredients:
- 5 ½ lb. ham, bone-in & cooked
- 1 cup apple cider
- ½ cup dark brown sugar
- 1/3 cup bourbon
- ¼ cup honey
- ¼ cup Dijon mustard
- 4 sprigs fresh thyme

Directions:
1. Place the ham in the cooking pot.
2. In a small bowl, whisk together cider, brown sugar, bourbon, honey, and mustard until smooth. Pour over the ham. Scatter the thyme around the ham.
3. Add the lid and set to slow cook on low. Cook 8 hours or until ham is very tender. Transfer ham to cutting board and let rest 10-15 minutes.
4. Pour the cooking liquid through fine mesh sieve into a bowl. Pour back into the cooking pot. Set to sauté on med-high heat and bring to a simmer, cook 10 minutes or until reduced, stirring occasionally.
5. Slice the ham and serve topped with sauce.

Nutrition Info:
- InfoCalories 372,Total Fat 10g,Total Carbs 20g,Protein 45g,Sodium 2000mg.

Pork Pie

Servings: 8
Cooking Time: 45 Minutes
Ingredients:
- 2 tablespoons extra-virgin olive oil
- 1 pound ground pork
- 1 yellow onion, diced
- 1 can black beans, drained
- 1 cup frozen corn kernels
- 1 can green chiles
- 2 tablespoons chili powder
- 1 box cornbread mix
- 1½ cups milk
- 1 cup shredded Cheddar cheese

Directions:
1. Select SEAR/SAUTÉ and set temperature to MED. Select START/STOP to begin. Let preheat for 3 minutes.
2. Add the olive oil, pork, and onion. Brown the pork, stirring frequently to break the meat into smaller pieces, until cooked through, about 5 minutes.
3. Add the beans, corn, chiles, and chili powder and stir. Simmer, stirring frequently, about 10 minutes.
4. In a medium bowl, combine the cornbread mix, milk, and cheese. Pour it over simmering mixture in an even layer. Close crisping lid.
5. Select BAKE/ROAST, set temperature to 360°F, and set time for 25 minutes. Select START/STOP to begin.
6. After 20 minutes, use wooden toothpick to check if cornbread is done. If the toothpick inserted into the cornbread does not come out clean, close lid and cook for the remaining 5 minutes.
7. When cooking is complete, open lid. Let cool for 10 minutes before slicing and serving.

Nutrition Info:
- InfoCalories: 491, Total Fat: 24g, Sodium: 667mg, Carbohydrates: 47g, Protein: 24g.

One Pot Ham & Rice

Servings: 4
Cooking Time: 10 Minutes
Ingredients:
- 2 tbsp. water
- ¼ cup celery, chopped
- ¼ cup onion, chopped
- ¼ cup green bell pepper, chopped
- ¼ cup fresh parsley, chopped
- ½ tsp garlic powder
- ¼ tsp pepper
- Nonstick cooking spray
- 5 slices lean deli ham, chopped
- 2 cups brown rice, cooked
- 2 eggs, beaten
- 1 green onion, sliced

Directions:
1. Add water to the cooking pot and set to sauté on medium heat.
2. Add the celery, onion, peppers, parsley, garlic powder, and pepper and cook until water evaporates and vegetables are tender, about 4-5 minutes.
3. Spray the vegetables and pot with cooking spray. Add ham and cook 1-2 minutes until heated through.
4. Stir in rice and mix well. Pour in eggs and cook until they are completely set, stirring occasionally.
5. Sprinkle with green onions and serve immediately.

Nutrition Info:
- InfoCalories 184, Total Fat 4g, Total Carbs 25g, Protein 11g, Sodium 413mg.

Chunky Pork Meatloaf With Mashed Potatoes

Servings: 4
Cooking Time: 55 Min
Ingredients:

- 2 pounds potatoes; cut into large chunks /900g
- 12 ounces pork meatloaf /360g
- 2 garlic cloves; minced
- 2 large eggs
- 12 individual saltine crackers, crushed
- 1¾ cups full cream milk; divided /438ml
- 1 cup chopped white onion /130g
- ½ cup heavy cream /125ml
- ¼ cup barbecue sauce /62.5ml
-
- 1 tbsp olive oil /15ml
- 3 tbsp chopped fresh cilantro /45g
- 3 tbsp unsalted butter /45g
- ¼ tsp dried rosemary /1.25g
- 1 tsp yellow mustard /5g
- 1 tsp Worcestershire sauce /5ml
- 2 tsp salt /10g
- ½ tsp black pepper /2.5g

Directions:
1. Select Sear/Sauté and adjust to Medium. Press Start to preheat the pot for 5 minutes. Heat the olive oil until shimmering and sauté the onion and garlic in the oil. Cook for about 2 minutes until the onion softens. Transfer the onion and garlic to a plate and set aside.
2. In a bowl, crumble the meatloaf mix into small pieces. Sprinkle with 1 tsp of salt, the pepper, cilantro, and thyme. Add the sautéed onion and garlic. Sprinkle the crushed saltine crackers over the meat and seasonings.
3. In a small bowl, beat ¼ cup of milk, the eggs, mustard, and Worcestershire sauce. Pour the mixture on the layered cracker crumbs and gently mix the ingredients in the bowl with your hands. Shape the meat mixture into an 8-inch round.
4. Cover the reversible rack with aluminum foil and carefully lift the meatloaf into the rack. Pour the remaining 1½ cups of milk and the heavy cream into the inner pot. Add the potatoes, butter, and remaining salt. Place the rack with meatloaf over the potatoes in the upper position in the pot.
5. Seal the pressure lid, choose Pressure; adjust the pressure to High and the cook time to 25 minutes; press Start. After cooking, perform a quick pressure release, and carefully open the pressure lid. Brush the meatloaf with the barbecue sauce.
6. Close the crisping lid; choose Broil and adjust the cook time to 7 minutes. Press Start to begin grilling. When the top has browned, remove the rack, and transfer the meatloaf to a serving platter. Mash the potatoes in the pot. Slice the meatloaf and serve with the mashed potatoes.

Beef And Bell Pepper With Onion Sauce

Servings: 6
Cooking Time: 62 Min
Ingredients:

- 2 lb. round steak pieces, about 6 to 8 pieces /900g
- ½ yellow bell pepper, finely chopped
- 1 yellow onion, finely chopped
- 2 cloves garlic; minced
- ½ green bell pepper, finely chopped
-
- ½ red bell pepper, finely chopped
- ¼ cup flour /32.5g
- ½ cup water /125ml
- 2 tbsp olive oil /30ml
- Salt and pepper, to taste

Directions:
1. Wrap the steaks in plastic wrap, place on a cutting board, and use a rolling pin to pound flat of about 2-inch thickness. Remove the plastic wrap and season them with salt and pepper. Set aside.
2. Put the chopped peppers, onion, and garlic in a bowl, and mix them evenly. Spoon the bell pepper mixture onto the flattened steaks and roll them to have the peppers inside.
3. Use some toothpicks to secure the beef rolls and dredge the steaks in all-purpose flour while shaking off any excess flour. Place them in a plate.
4. Select Sear/Sauté mode on Foodi and heat the oil. Add the beef rolls and brown them on both sides, for about 6 minutes.
5. Pour the water over the meat, close the lid, secure the pressure valve, and select Pressure mode on High pressure for 20 minutes. Press Start/Stop.
6. Once the timer has stopped, do a natural pressure release for 10 minutes. Close the crisping lid and cook for 10 minutes on Broil mode. When ready, Remove the meat to a plate and spoon the sauce from the pot over. Serve the stuffed meat rolls with a side of steamed veggies.

Pepper Crusted Tri Tip Roast

Servings: 6
Cooking Time: 45 Minutes
Ingredients:

- 1 tbsp. salt
- 1 tbsp. pepper
- 1 tbsp. garlic powder
- 1 tbsp. onion powder
- 1 tsp cayenne pepper
- 1 tbsp. oregano
- 1 tsp rosemary
- ½ tsp sage
- 3 lb. tri-tip roast
- Nonstick cooking spray

Directions:
1. In a small bowl, combine all the spices until mixed.
2. Place the roast on baking sheet and massage the rub mix into all sides. Cover and let sit 1 hour.
3. Lightly spray the cooking pot with cooking spray. Set to sear.
4. Add the roast and brown all sides. Add the tender-crisp lid and set to roast on 300°F.
5. Cook until meat thermometer reaches desired temperature for doneness, 120°F for a rare roast, 130°F for medium-rare and 140°F for medium, about 20-40 minutes.
6. Remove roast from cooking pot, tent with foil and let rest 10-15 minutes. Slice across the grain and serve.

Nutrition Info:
- InfoCalories 169,Total Fat 8g,Total Carbs 7g,Protein 19g,Sodium 2300mg.

Braised Lamb Shanks

Servings:4
Cooking Time: 4 Hours 15 Minutes
Ingredients:

- 2 bone-in lamb shanks, 2 to 2½ pounds each
- Kosher salt
- Freshly ground black pepper
- 2 tablespoons canola oil
- 2 Yukon gold potatoes, cut into 1-inch pieces
- 2 carrots, cut into 2-inch pieces
- 2 parsnips, peeled and cut into 2-inch pieces
- 1 bag frozen pearl onions
- 1 bottle red wine
- 1 cup chicken stock
- 1 tablespoon chopped fresh rosemary

Directions:
1. Select SEAR/SAUTÉ and set to HI. Select START/STOP to begin. Let preheat for 5 minutes.
2. Season the lamb shanks with salt and pepper.
3. Add the oil and lamb. Cook for 5 minutes on one side, then turn and cook for an additional 5 minutes. Remove the lamb and set aside.
4. Add the potatoes, carrots, parsnips, and pearl onions. Cook for 5 minutes, stirring occasionally.
5. Stir in the red wine, chicken stock, and rosemary. Add the lamb back to the pot and press down on the shanks to ensure they are mostly submerged in liquid. Assemble pressure lid, making sure the pressure release valve is in the VENT position.
6. Select SLOW COOK and set to HI. Set time to 4 hours. Select START/STOP to begin.
7. When cooking is complete, remove lid and serve.

Nutrition Info:
- InfoCalories: 791,Total Fat: 34g,Sodium: 591mg,Carbohydrates: 47g,Protein: 51g.

Calzones With Sausage And Mozzarella

Servings: 4
Cooking Time: 35 Min

Ingredients:
- 1 pound frozen bread dough /450g
- 1 small green bell pepper, seeded and chopped
- 2 or 3 Italian sausages
- ¼ cup tomato sauce /62.5ml
- 1 cup shredded mozzarella cheese /130g
- 2 tbsp olive oil/30ml

Directions:
1. On your Foodi, choose Sear/Sauté, and adjust to Medium-High to preheat the inner pot. Press Start to preheat the pot. Heat 1 tbsp of olive oil in the pot and sauté the bell pepper for 1 minute or until just starting to soften. Remove the pepper into a plate and set aside. Brown the sausages for 2 to 3 minutes on one side. Turn the sausages and brown the other side.
2. Add ¾ cup of water to the inner pot. Then, lock the pressure lid into place and set to seal. Choose Pressure; adjust the pressure to High and the cook time to 4 minutes. Press Start. After cooking, perform a quick pressure release and carefully open the pressure lid.
3. Remove the sausages from the pot onto a cutting board and cool for several minutes. Discard the water in the pot, wipe the pot dry with a clean napkin, and return the pot to the base. When the sausages have cooled, slice into ¼-inch rounds.
4. Cut four pieces of parchment paper about 8 inches and divide the dough into four equal pieces. One at a time and on a piece of parchment, use your hands to press each dough into a circle about 6 to 7 inches in diameter.
5. Close the crisping lid. Choose Bake/Roast and adjust the temperature to 400°F or 205°C. Press Start to preheat the pot for 5 minutes.
6. While the preheats, make the calzones. One after the other, spread 1 tbsp of tomato sauce over half a dough circle, leaving a ½-inch clear border. Arrange the sausage rounds in a single layer and sprinkle a quarter of the green peppers over the top.
7. Top with a quarter cup of cheese. Use the parchment to pull the other side of the dough over the filling and pinch the edges together to seal. Repeat the process with another dough.
8. Cut the parchment around each calzone, so it is about ½ inch larger than the calzone. Brush the calzones with some of the remaining olive oil. With a large spatula, transfer the two calzones to the reversible rack set in the lower position in the pot. Open the lid and place the rack in the pot.
9. Close the crisping lid and choose Bake/Roast; adjust the temperature to 400°F or 205°C and the cook time to 12 minutes. Press Start.
10. After 6 minutes, check the calzones, which will be a dark golden brown. Remove the rack and turn the calzones over. Remove the parchment paper and brush the tops with a little olive oil. Return the rack to the pot. Close the lid and continue cooking for the last 6 minutes.
11. While the first two calzones bake, assemble the remaining two. When the first set of calzones are done, transfer to a wire rack to cool and bake the second batch.

Ham, Ricotta & Zucchini Fritters

Servings: 4
Cooking Time: 10 Minutes
Ingredients:
- 1 ½ tbsp. butter, unsalted
- 1/3 cup milk
- ½ cup ricotta cheese
- 2 eggs
- 1 ½ tsp baking powder
- ½ tsp salt
- ¼ tsp pepper
- 1 cup flour
- ¼ cup fresh basil, chopped
- 3 oz. ham, cut in strips
- ½ zucchini, cut into matchsticks

Directions:
1. Spray the fryer basket with cooking spray. Place in the cooking pot.
2. Place the butter in a large microwave safe bowl and microwave until melted.
3. Whisk milk and ricotta into melted butter until smooth. Whisk in eggs until combined.
4. Stir in baking powder, salt, and pepper until combined. Stir in flour, until combined.
5. Fold in basil, ham and zucchini until distributed evenly. Drop batter by ¼ cups into fryer basket, these will need to be cooked in batches.
6. Add the tender-crisp lid and set to air fry on 375°F. Cook fritters 4-5 minutes per side until golden brown and cooked through. Serve immediately.

Nutrition Info:
- InfoCalories 180, Total Fat 10g, Total Carbs 15g, Protein 7g, Sodium 451mg.

Braised Short Ribs With Creamy Sauce

Servings: 6
Cooking Time: 1 Hr 55 Min
Ingredients:
- 3 pounds beef short ribs /1350g
- 1 can diced tomatoes /435g
- 1 celery stalk; chopped
- 3 garlic cloves; chopped
- 1 onion; chopped
- 1 large carrot; chopped
- 2 cups beef broth /500ml
- ½ cup cheese cream /65g
- ½ cup dry red wine /125ml
- ¼ cup red wine vinegar /62.5ml
- 2 bay leaves
- 2 tbsp olive oil /30ml
- 2 tbsp chopped parsley /30g
- ¼ tsp red pepper flakes /1.25g
- 2 tsp salt; divided /10g
- 1½ tsp freshly ground black pepper; divided /7.5g

Directions:
1. Season your short ribs with 1 tsp black pepper and 1 tsp salt. Warm olive oil on Sear/Sauté. Add in short ribs and sear for 3 minutes each side until browned. Set aside on a bowl.
2. Drain everything only to be left with 1 tbsp of the remaining fat from the pot. Set on Sear/Sauté, and stir-fry garlic, carrot, onion, and celery in the hot fat for 4 to 6 minutes until fragrant.
3. Stir in broth, wine, red pepper flakes, vinegar, tomatoes, bay leaves, and remaining pepper and salt; turn the Foodi to Sear/Sauté on Low and bring the mixture to a boil.
4. With the bone-side up, lay short ribs into the braising liquid. Seal the pressure lid, choose Pressure, set to High, and set the timer to 40 minutes. Press Start.
5. When ready, release the pressure quickly. Set the short ribs on a plate. Get rid of bay leaves. Skim and get rid of the fat from the surface of braising liquid.
6. Using an immersion blender, blend the liquid for 1 minute; add cream cheese, pepper and salt and blitz until smooth Arrange the ribs onto a serving plate, pour the sauce over and top with parsley.

Cuban Pork

Servings: 8
Cooking Time: 2 Hr 30 Min

Ingredients:
- 3 pounds pork shoulder /1350g
- ¼ cup lime juice /62.5ml
- ½ cup orange juice /125ml
- ¼ cup canola oil /62.5ml
- ¼ cup chopped fresh cilantro /32.5g
- 8 cloves garlic; minced
- 1 tbsp fresh oregano /15g
- 1 tbsp ground cumin /15g
- 1 tsp red pepper flakes /5g
- 2 tsp ground black pepper /10g
- 1 tsp salt /5g

Directions:
1. In a bowl, mix orange juice, olive oil, cumin, salt, pepper, oregano, lime juice, and garlic; add into a large plastic bag alongside the pork. Seal and massage the bag to ensure the marinade covers the pork completely.
2. Place in the refrigerator for an hour to overnight. In the Foodi, set your removed pork from bag. Add the marinade on top. Seal the pressure lid, choose Pressure, set to High, and set the timer to 50 minutes. Press Start.
3. Release pressure naturally for 15 minutes. Transfer the pork to a cutting board; use a fork to break into smaller pieces.
4. Skim and get rid of the fat from liquid in the cooker. Serve the liquid with pork and sprinkle with cilantro.

Handwritten notes:

1 - 1.3 kg shoulder pork; cubed
3 tbs BBQ Seasoning
1 tbs garlic powder
2 tsp Sea Salt
200 ml cider vinegar
170 tomato paste

High pressure 35 mins = Pork Spice/vinegar
Quick release
Sear Saute : MID-HI. Add tomato paste
Simmer 10 mins reduce liquid

Bake/Roast 180°C 10 mins

Fish & Seafood

Cod Cornflakes Nuggets

Servings: 4
Cooking Time: 25 Min
Ingredients:
- 1 ¼ lb. cod fillets, cut into chunks /662.5g
- 1 egg
- 1 cup cornflakes /130g
- ½ cup flour /65g
- 1 tbsp olive oil/15ml
- 1 tbsp water /15ml
- Salt and pepper, to taste

Directions:
1. Add the oil and cornflakes in a food processor, and process until crumbed. Season the fish chunks with salt and pepper.
2. Beat the egg along with 1 tbsp or 15ml water. Dredge the chunks in flour first, then dip in the egg, and coat with cornflakes. Arrange on a lined sheet. Close the crisping lid and cook at 350 °F or 177°C for 15 minutes on Air Crisp mode.

Shrimp Egg Rolls

Servings: 10
Cooking Time: 10 Minutes
Ingredients:
- Nonstick cooking spray
- ¼ cup soy sauce, low sodium
- 2 tbsp. brown sugar
- 1 tsp ginger, grated
- 1 tsp garlic powder
- 5 cups coleslaw mix
- 2 green onions, sliced thin
- 3 tbsp. cilantro, chopped
- 1 cup small shrimp, chopped
- 10 egg roll wrappers

Directions:
1. Spray the fryer basket with cooking spray.
2. In a small bowl, whisk together, soy sauce, brown sugar, ginger, and garlic powder until combined.
3. In a large bowl, combine coleslaw, green onions, cilantro, and shrimp and mix well.
4. Pour the soy sauce over the coleslaw and toss well to coat. Let sit 15 minutes. After 15 minutes, place in a colander and squeeze to remove as much liquid as possible.
5. Place egg roll wrappers on a work surface. Spoon about 1/3 cup of shrimp mixture in the center of each wrapper. Fold opposite sides over filling, then one corner and roll up egg roll fashion. Place seam side down in fryer basket and spray lightly with cooking spray.
6. Add the tender-crisp lid and set to air fry on 425°F. Cook 8-10 minutes until golden brown and crisp, turning over halfway through cooking time.

Nutrition Info:
- InfoCalories 138,Total Fat 1g,Total Carbs 24g,Protein 7g,Sodium 532mg.

Tuna Zoodle Bake

Servings: 4
Cooking Time: 20 Minutes
Ingredients:
- Nonstick cooking spray
- 2 zucchini, cut in noodles with a spiralizer
- 1tsp olive oil
- ¼ cup onion, chopped fine
- 6 oz. tuna, drained
- ½ tbsp. tomato paste
- ½ cup tomatoes, diced & drained
- ¼ cup skim milk
- ½ tsp thyme
- ¼ tsp salt
- ¼ tsp pepper
- 1/8 cup parmesan cheese, fat free
- 1/4 cup cheddar cheese, reduced fat, grated

Directions:
1. Spray an 8x8-inch baking pan with cooking spray.
2. Place the zucchini in an even layer in the prepared pan.
3. Add the oil to the cooking pot and set to sauté on med-high heat. Once the oil is hot, add the onion and cook 2 minutes, or until soft.
4. Stir in the tuna and tomato paste and cook 1 minute more. Add the tomatoes, milk, thyme, salt, and pepper and bring to a low simmer. Stir in parmesan cheese and cook until it melts.
5. Pour the tuna mixture over the zucchini and sprinkle cheddar cheese over the top. Wipe out the pat and place the baking pan in it.
6. Add the tender-crisp lid and set to bake on 400°F. Bake 15 minutes until cheese is melted and bubbly. Serve.

Nutrition Info:
- InfoCalories 80,Total Fat 3g,Total Carbs 2g,Protein 11g,Sodium 371mg.

Caramelized Salmon

Servings: 4
Cooking Time: 10 Minutes
Ingredients:
- 1 tbsp. coconut oil, melted
- 1/3 cup Stevia brown sugar, packed
- 3 tbsp. fish sauce
- 1 ½ tbsp. soy sauce
- 1 tsp fresh ginger, peeled & grated
- 2 tsp lime zest, finely grated
- 1 tbsp. fresh lime juice
- ½ tsp pepper
- 4 salmon fillets
- 1 tbsp. green onions, sliced
- 1 tbsp. cilantro chopped

Directions:
1. Add the oil, brown sugar, fish sauce, soy sauce, ginger, zest, juice, and pepper to the cooking pot. Stir to mix.
2. Set to sauté on medium heat and bring mixture to a simmer, stirring frequently. Turn heat off.
3. Add the fish to the sauce making sure it is covered. Add the lid and set to pressure cooking on low. Set the timer for 1 minute.
4. When the timer goes off let the pressure release naturally for 5 minutes, the release it manually. Fish is done when it flakes with a fork.
5. Transfer fish to a serving dish with the caramelized side up.
6. Set cooker back to sauté on medium and cook sauce 3-4 minutes until it's thickened. Spoon over fish and garnish with chopped green onions and scallions. Serve.

Nutrition Info:
- InfoCalories 316,Total Fat 18g,Total Carbs 5g,Protein 35g,Sodium 1514mg.

Seafood Gumbo

Servings: 4
Cooking Time: 90 Min

Ingredients:

- 1 pound jumbo shrimp /450g
- 8 ounces lump crabmeat /240g
- 1 medium onion; chopped
- 2 green onions, finely sliced
- 1 small banana pepper, seeded and minced
- 1 small red bell pepper; chopped (about ⅔ cup)
- 2 celery stalks; chopped
- 2 garlic cloves, minced
- 3 cups chicken broth /750ml
- ¼ cup olive oil, plus 2 tsp s /72.5ml
- ⅓ cup all-purpose flour /44g
- 1 cup jasmine rice /130g
- ¾ cup water /375ml
- 1½ tsp s Cajun Seasoning /7.5g
- 1½ tsp s salt divided /7.5g

Directions:

1. Lay the shrimp in the Crisping Basket. Season with ½ tsp or 2.5g of salt and 2 tsp s or 10ml of olive oil. Toss to coat and fix the basket in the inner pot. Close the crisping lid and Choose Air Crisp; adjust the temperature to 400°F or 205°C and the cook time to 6 minutes. Press Start.
2. After 3 minutes, open the lid and toss the shrimp. Close the lid and resume cooking. When ready, the shrimp should be opaque and pink. Remove the basket and set aside.
3. Choose Sear/Sauté and adjust to High. Press Start. Heat the remaining ¼ cup of olive oil. Whisk in the flour with a wooden spoon and cook the roux that forms for 3 to 5 minutes, stirring constantly, until the roux has the color of peanut butter. Turn the pot off.
4. Stir in the Cajun, onion, bell pepper, celery, garlic, and banana pepper for about 5 minutes until the mixture slightly cools. Add the chicken broth and crabmeat, stir.
5. Put the rice into a heatproof bowl. Add the water and the remaining salt. Cover the bowl with foil. Put the reversible rack in the lower position of the pot and set the bowl in the rack.
6. Seal the pressure lid, choose Pressure; adjust the pressure to High and the cook time to 6 minutes; press Start. After cooking, perform a natural pressure for 8 minutes. Take out the rack and bowl and set aside. Stir the shrimp into the gumbo to heat it up for 3 minutes.
7. Fluff the rice with a fork and divide into the center of four bowls. Spoon the gumbo around the rice and garnish with the green onions.

Pepper Smothered Cod

Servings: 4
Cooking Time: 20 Minutes

Ingredients:

- ¼ cup olive oil
- ½ cup red onion, chopped
- 2 tsp garlic, chopped
- ½ cup red bell pepper, chopped
- ½ cup green bell pepper, chopped
- Salt and pepper, to taste
- 4 tbsp. flour
- 2 cups chicken broth, low sodium
- ½ cup tomato, seeded & chopped
- 2 tsp fresh thyme, chopped
- 4 cod filets

Directions:

1. Set to sauté on med-high heat and add oil to the cooking pot.
2. Add the onion and garlic and cook, stirring, 1 minute.
3. Add the peppers, salt, and pepper and cook, stirring frequently about 2-3 minutes, or until peppers start to get tender.
4. Stir in the flour and cook until it turns a light brown.
5. Pour in the broth and cook, stirring, until smooth and the sauce starts to thicken. Stir in tomato and thyme.
6. Season the fish with salt and pepper. Place in the pot and add the lid. Cook 3-4 minutes, then turn the fish over and cook another 3-4 minute or until fish flakes easily with a fork. Transfer the fish to serving plates and top with sauce. Serve immediately.

Nutrition Info:

- InfoCalories 249,Total Fat 14g,Total Carbs 11g,Protein 19g,Sodium 1107mg.

Coconut Shrimp

Servings: 2
Cooking Time: 30 Min
Ingredients:
- 8 large shrimp
- ½ cup orange jam /65g
- ½ cup shredded coconut /65g
- ½ cup breadcrumbs /65g
- 8 oz. coconut milk /240ml
- 1 tbsp honey /15ml
- ½ tsp cayenne pepper/2.5g
- ¼ tsp hot sauce /1.25ml
- 1 tsp mustard /5g
- ¼ tsp salt /1.25g
- ¼ tsp pepper /1.25g

Directions:
1. Combine the breadcrumbs, cayenne pepper, shredded coconut, salt, and pepper in a small bowl. Dip the shrimp in the coconut milk, first, and then in the coconut crumbs.
2. Arrange in the lined Ninja Foodi basket, close the crisping lid and cook for 20 minutes on Air Crisp mode at 350 °F or 177°C.
3. Meanwhile whisk the jam, honey, hot sauce, and mustard. Serve the shrimp with the sauce.

Mustard And Apricot-glazed Salmon With Smashed Potatoes

Servings:4
Cooking Time: 25 Minutes
Ingredients:
- 20 ounces baby potatoes, whole
- 1½ cups water
- 4 frozen skinless salmon fillets
- ¼ cup apricot preserves
- 2 teaspoons Dijon mustard
- 2 tablespoons extra-virgin olive oil
- ½ teaspoon kosher salt
- ½ teaspoon freshly ground black pepper

Directions:
1. Place the potatoes and water in the pot. Put Reversible Rack in pot, making sure it is in the higher position. Place salmon on the rack. Assemble pressure lid, making sure the pressure release valve is in the SEAL position.
2. Select PRESSURE and set to HI. Set time to 5 minutes. Select START/STOP to begin.
3. Mix together the apricot preserves and mustard in a small bowl.
4. When pressure cooking is complete, quick release the pressure by turning the pressure release valve to the VENT position. Carefully remove lid when unit has finished releasing pressure.
5. Carefully remove rack with salmon. Remove potatoes from pot and drain. Place the potatoes on a cutting board and, using the back of a knife, carefully press down to flatten each. Drizzle the flattened potatoes with the olive oil and season with salt and pepper.
6. Place Cook & Crisp Basket in the pot. Place the potatoes into the basket and close crisping lid.
7. Select AIR CRISP, set temperature to 390°F, and set time to 15 minutes. Select START/STOP to begin.
8. After 8 minutes, open lid, and using silicone-tipped tongs, gently flip the potatoes. Lower basket back into pot and close lid to resume cooking.
9. When cooking is complete, remove basket from pot. Return the rack with the salmon to the pot, making sure the rack is in the higher position. Gently brush the salmon with the apricot and mustard mixture.
10. Close crisping lid. Select BROIL and set time to 5 minutes. Select START/STOP to begin.
11. When cooking is complete, remove salmon and serve immediately with the potatoes.

Nutrition Info:
- InfoCalories: 359,Total Fat: 11g,Sodium: 711mg,Carbohydrates: 36g,Protein: 31g.

Classic Crab Imperial

Servings: 6
Cooking Time: 20 Minutes

Ingredients:
- 1 cup mayonnaise
- 2 eggs, lightly beaten
- 2 tsp sugar
- 2 tsp Old Bay seasoning
- 1 tsp lemon juice
- 2 tsp parsley, chopped fine
- 2 lb. jumbo lump crab meat

Directions:
1. In a medium bowl, combine mayonnaise, eggs, sugar, Old Bay, lemon juice, and parsley and mix well.
2. Gently fold in crab. Divide evenly between 6 ramekins and place in the cooking pot.
3. Add the tender-crisp lid and set to bake on 350°F. Bake 20-25 minutes until the top is golden brown. Let cool slightly before serving.

Nutrition Info:
- InfoCalories 382,Total Fat 18g,Total Carbs 10g,Protein 43g,Sodium 1201mg.

Chorizo And Shrimp Boil

Servings: 4
Cooking Time: 30 Min

Ingredients:
- 4 chorizo sausages; sliced
- 1 pound shrimp, peeled and deveined /450g
- 1 lemon, cut into wedges
- 3 red potatoes
- 3 ears corn, cut into 1½-inch rounds
- ¼ cup butter, melted /62.5ml
- 1 cup white wine /250ml
- 2 cups water /500ml
- 2 tbsp of seafood seasoning /30g
- salt to taste

Directions:
1. To your Foodi add all Ingredients except butter and lemon wedges. Do not stir. Seal the pressure lid, choose Pressure, set to High, and set the timer to 2 minutes; press Start. When ready, release the pressure quickly.
2. Drain the mixture through a colander. Transfer to a serving platter. Serve with melted butter and lemon wedges.

Mussel Chowder With Oyster Crackers

Servings: 4
Cooking Time: 75 Min

Ingredients:

- 1 pound parsnips, peeled and cut into chunks /450g
- 3 cans chopped mussels, drained, liquid reserved /180g
- 1½ cups heavy cream /375ml
- 2 cups oyster crackers /260g
- ¼ cup white wine /62.5ml
- ¼ cup finely grated Pecorino Romano cheese/32.5g
- 1 cup clam juice /130g
- 2 thick pancetta slices, cut into thirds
- 1 bay leaf
- 2 celery stalks; chopped
- 1 medium onion; chopped
- 1 tbsp flour /15g
- 2 tbsps chopped fresh chervil/30g
- 2 tbsps melted ghee /30g
- ½ tsp garlic powder /2.5g
- 1 tsp salt; divided /5g
- 1 tsp dried rosemary /5g

Directions:

1. To preheat the Foodi, close the crisping lid and Choose Air Crisp; adjust the temperature to 375°F or 191°C and the time to 2 minutes; press Start. In a bowl, pour in the oyster crackers. Drizzle with the melted ghee, add the cheese, garlic powder, and ½ tsp or 2.5g of salt. Toss to coat the crackers. Transfer to the crisping basket.
2. Once the pot is ready, open the pressure lid and fix the basket in the pot. Close the lid and Choose Air Crisp; adjust the temperature to 375°F or 191°C and the cook time to 6 minutes; press Start.
3. After 3 minutes, carefully open the lid and mix the crackers with a spoon. Close the lid and resume cooking until crisp and lightly browned. Take out the basket and set aside to cool.
4. On the pot, choose Sear/Sauté and adjust to Medium. Press Start. Add the pancetta and cook for 5 minutes, turning once or twice, until crispy.
5. Remove the pancetta to a paper towel-lined plate to drain fat; set aside.
6. Sauté the celery and onion in the pancetta grease for 1 minute or until the vegetables start softening. Mix the flour into the vegetables to coat evenly and pour the wine over the veggies. Cook for about 1 minute or until reduced by about one-third.
7. Pour in the clam juice, the reserved mussel liquid, parsnips, remaining salt, rosemary, and bay leaf. Seal the pressure lid, choose Pressure; adjust the pressure to High and the cook time to 4 minutes. Press Start.
8. After cooking, perform a natural pressure release for 5 minutes. Stir in the mussels and heavy cream. Choose Sear/Sauté and adjust to Medium. Press Start to simmer to the chowder and heat the mussels. Carefully remove and discard the bay leaf after.
9. Spoon the soup into bowls and crumble the pancetta over the top. Garnish with the chervil and a handful of oyster crackers, serving the remaining crackers on the side.

Steamed Sea Bass With Turnips

Servings: 4
Cooking Time: 15 Min
Ingredients:
- 4 sea bass fillets
- 4 sprigs thyme
- 1 lemon; sliced
- 2 turnips; sliced
- 1 white onion; sliced into thin rings
- 1½ cups water /375ml
- 2 tsp olive oil /30ml
- 2 pinches salt
- 1 pinch ground black pepper

Directions:
1. Add water to the Foodi. Set a reversible rack into the pot. Line a parchment paper to the bottom of steamer basket. Place lemon slices in a single layer on the reversible rack.
2. Arrange fillets on the top of the lemons, cover with onion and thyme sprigs and top with turnip slices.
3. Drizzle pepper, salt, and olive oil over the mixture. Put steamer basket onto the reversible rack. Seal lid and cook on Low for 8 minutes; press Start.
4. When ready, release pressure quickly. Serve over the delicate onion rings and thinly sliced turnips.

Penne All Arrabbiata With Seafood And Chorizo

Servings: 4
Cooking Time: 50 Min
Ingredients:
- 16 ounces penne /480g
- 8 ounces shrimp, peeled and deveined /240g
- 8 ounces scallops /240g
- 12 clams, cleaned and debearded
- 1 jar Arrabbiata sauce /720ml
- 1 onion; diced
- 3 cups fish broth /750ml
- 1 chorizo; sliced
- 1 tbsp olive oil /15ml
- ½ tsp freshly ground black pepper /2.5g
- ½ tsp salt /2.5g

Directions:
1. Choose Sear/Sauté on the pot and set to Medium High. Choose Start/Stop to preheat the pot. Heat the oil and add the chorizo, onion, and garlic; sauté them for about 5 minutes. Stir in the penne, Arrabbiata sauce, and broth.
2. Season with the black pepper and salt and mix. Seal the pressure lid, choose Pressure, set to High and set the time to 2 minutes; press Start. When the time is over, do a quick pressure release and carefully open the lid.
3. Choose Sear/Sauté and set to Medium High. Choose Start/Stop. Stir in the shrimp, scallops, and clams. Put the pressure lid together and set to the Vent position.
4. Cover and cook for 5 minutes, until the clams have opened and the shrimp and scallops are opaque and cooked through.
5. Discard any unopened clams. Spoon the seafood and chorizo pasta into serving bowls and serve warm.

Salmon With Dill Sauce

Servings: 4
Cooking Time: 20-25 Minutes

Ingredients:
- 4 salmon, each of 6 ounces
- 2 teaspoons olive oil
- 1 pinch salt
- Dill Sauce
- 1/2 cup non-Fat: Greek Yogurt
- 1/2 cup sour cream
- Pinch of salt
- 2 tablespoons dill, chopped

Directions:
1. Preheat Ninja Foodi by pressing the "AIR CRISP" option and setting it to "270 °F" and timer to 25 minutes.
2. Wait until the appliance beeps.
3. Drizzle cut pieces of salmon with 1 teaspoon olive oil.
4. Season with salt.
5. Take the cooking basket out and transfer salmon to basket, cook for 20-23 minutes.
6. Take a suitable and stir in sour cream, salt, chopped dill, yogurt and mix well to prepare the dill sauce.
7. Serve cooked salmon by pouring the sauce all over.
8. Garnish with chopped dill and enjoy.

Nutrition Info:
- InfoCalories: 600; Fat: 45g; Carbohydrates: 5g; Protein: 60g

Sweet & Spicy Shrimp

Servings: 4
Cooking Time: 5 Minutes

Ingredients:
- ¾ cup pineapple juice, unsweetened
- 1 red bell pepper, sliced
- 1 ½ cups cauliflower, grated
- ¼ cup dry white wine
- ½ cup water
- 2 tbsp. soy sauce
- 2 tbsp. Thai sweet chili sauce
- 1 tbsp. chili paste
- 1 lb. large shrimp, frozen
- 4 green onions, chopped, white & green separated
- 1 ½ cups pineapple chunks, drained

Directions:
1. Add ¾ cup pineapple juice along with remaining ingredients, except the pineapple chunks and green parts of the onion, to the cooking pot. Stir to mix.
2. Add the lid and set to pressure cook on high. Set timer for 2 minutes. When the timer goes off, release pressure 10 minutes before opening the pot.
3. Add the green parts of the onions and pineapple chunks and stir well. Serve immediately.

Nutrition Info:
- InfoCalories 196, Total Fat 1g, Total Carbs 22g, Protein 26g, Sodium 764mg.

Spicy Grilled Shrimp

Servings: 4
Cooking Time: 6 Minutes
Ingredients:
- 1 teaspoon garlic salt
- 1/2 teaspoon black pepper
- 1 tablespoon paprika
- 1 tablespoon garlic powder
- 2 tablespoons olive oil
- 1-pound jumbo shrimps, peeled and deveined
- 2 tablespoons brown erythritol

Directions:
1. Take a mixing bowl and stir in the listed ingredients to mix well.
2. Let it chill and marinate for 30-60 minutes.
3. Preheat Ninja Foodi by pressing the "GRILL" option and setting it to "MED" and timer to 6 minutes.
4. Let it preheat until you hear a beep.
5. Set prepared shrimps over grill grate, Lock and secure the Ninja Foodi's lid and cook for 3 minutes, flip and cook for 3 minutes more.
6. Serve and enjoy.

Nutrition Info:
- InfoCalories: 370; Fat: 27g; Carbohydrates: 23g; Protein: 6g

Tilapia & Tamari Garlic Mushrooms

Servings: 4
Cooking Time: 10 Minutes
Ingredients:
- 2 tbsp. sesame oil, divided
- 2 cloves garlic, chopped fine
- 2 cups mushrooms, sliced
- 4 tilapia fillets
- ½ tsp salt
- ¼ tsp pepper
- 1 tbsp. fresh lime juice
- 1 tbsp. tamari
- ¼ cup cilantro, chopped

Directions:
1. Add 1 tablespoon oil to the cooking pot and set to sauté on med-high heat.
2. Add the garlic and mushrooms and cook, stirring occasionally, 2-3 minutes.
3. Add the rack to the pot and top with a sheet of foil. Place the fish on the foil and brush with the remaining oil. Season with salt and pepper and drizzle lime juice over the tops.
4. Add the tender-crisp lid and set to roast on 350°F. Cook 5 minutes or until fish flakes with a fork and the liquid from the mushrooms has evaporated.
5. Transfer fish to serving plates. Stir the tamari into the mushrooms and spoon over fish. Garnish with cilantro and serve.

Nutrition Info:
- InfoCalories 298, Total Fat 12g, Total Carbs 2g, Protein 44g, Sodium 610mg.

Buttered Fish

Servings: 4
Cooking Time: 6 Minutes
Ingredients:
- 1-pound fish chunks
- 1 tablespoon vinegar
- 2 drops liquid stevia
- 1/4 cup butter
- Black pepper and salt to taste

Directions:
1. Select "Sauté" mode on your Ninja Foodi.
2. Stir in butter and melt it.
3. Add fish chunks, Sauté for 3 minutes.
4. Stir in stevia, salt, pepper, stir it.
5. Close the crisping lid.
6. Cook on "Air Crisp" mode for 3 minutes to 360 °F.
7. Serve and enjoy.

Nutrition Info:
- InfoCalories: 274g; Fat: 15g; Carbohydrates: 2g; Protein: 33g

Crab Bisque

Servings: 6
Cooking Time: 15 Minutes
Ingredients:
- 3 tbsp. butter
- 1 carrot, chopped fine
- 2 stalks celery, chopped fine
- 2 tbsp. flour
- 1 clove garlic, chopped fine
- 1 tbsp. fresh parsley, chopped
- 2 cups chicken broth, low sodium
- ½ cup sherry
- ¼ tsp pepper
- 18 oz. lump crab meat
- 2 cups half and half

Directions:
1. Add the butter to the cooking pot and set to sauté on medium heat.
2. Once the butter has melted, add the carrots and celery and cook 5-7 minutes until vegetables start to soften.
3. Sprinkle in the flour and cook, stirring, one minute. Add remaining ingredients, except crab and cream, and stir to combine.
4. Bring to a boil and cook one minute. Reduce heat to low and stir in crab and cream. Cook, stirring until bisque is heated through. Serve immediately.

Nutrition Info:
- InfoCalories 200,Total Fat 8g,Total Carbs 12g,Protein 18g,Sodium 770mg.

Salmon With Dill Chutney

Servings: 2
Cooking Time: 15 Min
Ingredients:
- 2 salmon fillets
- Juice from ½ lemon
- 2 cups water /500ml
- ¼ tsp paprika /1.25g
- salt and freshly ground pepper to taste
- For Chutney:
- ¼ cup extra virgin olive oil /62.5ml
- ¼ cup fresh dill /32.5g
- Juice from ½ lemon
- Sea salt to taste

Directions:
1. In a food processor, blend all the chutney Ingredients until creamy. Set aside. To your Foodi, add the water and place a reversible rack.
2. Arrange salmon fillets skin-side down on the steamer basket. Drizzle lemon juice over salmon and apply a seasoning of paprika.
3. Seal the pressure lid, choose Pressure, set to High, and set the timer to 3 minutes; press Start. When ready, release the pressure quickly. Season the fillets with pepper and salt, transfer to a serving plate and top with the dill chutney.

Spiced Red Snapper

Servings: 6
Cooking Time: 20 Minutes
Ingredients:
- Nonstick cooking spray
- 1 onion, sliced
- 14 ½ oz. stewed tomatoes, undrained, chopped
- 1/3 cup dry white wine
- 3 tbsp. fresh lemon juice
- 1 tsp cumin
- 1/8 tsp cinnamon
- 6 red snapper fillets

Directions:
1. Spray the cooking pot with cooking spray.
2. Set to sauté on med-high heat and add the onion. Cook, stirring, 3-4 minutes or until onions are soft.
3. Add tomatoes, wine, lemon juice, cumin,, and cinnamon and cook about 5 minutes or until sauce has thickened slightly.
4. Add the fish and spoon sauce over the top. Add the lid and reduce heat to medium. Cook 8-10 minutes until fish flakes with a fork.
5. Transfer fish to serving plates and top with sauce. Serve immediately.

Nutrition Info:
- InfoCalories 155,Total Fat 2g,Total Carbs 8g,Protein 25g,Sodium 201mg.

Panko Crusted Cod

Servings: 4
Cooking Time: 15 Minutes
Ingredients:
- 2 uncooked cod fillets
- 3 teaspoons kosher salt
- ¾ cup panko bread crumbs
- 2 tablespoons butter, melted
- 1/4 cup fresh parsley, minced
- 1 lemon. Zested and juiced

Directions:
1. Pre-heat your Ninja Foodi at 390 °F and place the Air Crisper basket inside.
2. Season cod and salt.
3. Take a suitable and stir in bread crumbs, parsley, lemon juice, zest, butter, and mix well.
4. Coat fillets with the bread crumbs mixture and place fillets in your Air Crisping basket.
5. Lock Air Crisping lid and cook on Air Crisp mode for 15 minutes at 360 °F.
6. Serve and enjoy.

Nutrition Info:
- InfoCalories: 554; Fat: 24g; Carbohydrates: 5g; Protein: 37g

Sesame Tuna Steaks

Servings: 4
Cooking Time: 10 Minutes
Ingredients:
- Nonstick cooking spray
- 2 tsp sesame oil
- 1 clove garlic, chopped fine
- 4 tuna steaks
- 1/8 tsp salt
- ½ tsp pepper
- ½ cup sesame seeds

Directions:
1. Place the rack in the cooking pot and spray it with cooking spray.
2. In a small bowl combine the oil and garlic. Rub it on both sides of the fish. Season with salt and pepper.
3. Place the sesame seeds in a shallow dish. Press the fish in the sesame seeds to coat completely. Place them on the rack.
4. Add the tender-crisp lid and set to roast on 350°F. Cook 8-10 minutes, turning over halfway through cooking time, until fish flakes with a fork. Serve immediately.

Nutrition Info:
- InfoCalories 263,Total Fat 14g,Total Carbs 3g,Protein 32g,Sodium 60mg.

Salmon, Cashew & Kale Bowl

Servings: 6
Cooking Time: 15 Minutes
Ingredients:
- 12 oz. salmon filets, skin off
- 2 tbsp. olive oil, divided
- ½ tsp salt
- ¼ tsp pepper
- 2 cloves garlic, chopped fine
- 4 cups kale, stems removed & chopped
- ½ cup carrot, grated
- 2 cups quinoa, cooked according to package directions
- ¼ cup cashews, chopped

Directions:
1. Place the rack in the cooking pot and set to bake on 400°F. Place a sheet of parchment paper on the rack.
2. Brush the salmon with 1 tablespoon of oil and season with salt and pepper. Place the fish on the parchment paper.
3. Add the tender-crisp lid and cook 15 minutes or until salmon reaches desired doneness. Transfer the fish to a plate and keep warm.
4. Set the cooker to sauté on medium heat and add the remaining oil. Once the oil is hot, add garlic, kale, and carrot and cook, stirring frequently, until kale is wilted and soft, about 2-3 minutes.
5. Add the quinoa and cashews and cook just until heated through. Spoon mixture evenly into bowl and top with a piece of salmon. Serve immediately.

Nutrition Info:
- InfoCalories 294,Total Fat 17g,Total Carbs 18g,Protein 17g,Sodium 243mg.

Tuna Patties

Servings: 2
Cooking Time: 50 Min
Ingredients:
- 5 oz. of canned tuna /150g
- 1 small onion; diced
- 2 eggs
- ¼ cup flour /32.5g
- ½ cup milk /125ml
- 1 tsp lime juice /5ml
- 1 tsp paprika /5g
- 1 tsp chili powder, optional /5g
- ½ tsp salt /2.5g

Directions:
1. Place all Ingredients in a bowl, and mix to combine. Make two large patties, or a few smaller ones, out of the mixture. Place them on a lined sheet and refrigerate for 30 minutes.
2. Close the crisping lid and cook the patties for about 6 minutes on each side on Roast mode at 350 °F or 177°C.

Vegan & Vegetable

Parsley Mashed Cauliflower

Servings: 4
Cooking Time: 15 Min
Ingredients:
- 1 head cauliflower
- 1/4 cup heavy cream /62.5g
- 2 cups water /500ml
- 1 tbsp fresh parsley, finely chopped /15g
- 1 tbsp butter /15g
- ¼ tsp celery salt /1.25g
- ⅛ tsp freshly ground black pepper /0.625g

Directions:
1. Into the pot, add water and set trivet on top and lay cauliflower head onto the trivet. Seal the pressure lid, choose Pressure, set to High, and set the timer to 8 minutes. Press Start.
2. When ready, release the pressure quickly. Remove the trivet and drain liquid from the pot before returning to the base.
3. Take back the cauliflower to the pot alongside the pepper, heavy cream, salt and butter; use an immersion blender to blend until smooth. Top with parsley and serve.

Red Beans And Rice

Servings: 4
Cooking Time: 1 Hr
Ingredients:
- 1 cup red beans, rinsed and stones removed /130g
- ½ cup rice, rinsed /65g
- 1 ½ cup vegetable broth /375ml
- 1 onion; diced
- 1 red bell pepper; diced
- 1 stalk celery; diced
- 1 tbsp fresh thyme leaves, or to taste /15g
- 2 tbsps olive oil /30ml
- ½ tsp cayenne pepper /2.5g
- water as needed
- salt and freshly ground black pepper to taste

Directions:
1. Into the pot, add beans and water to cover about 1-inch. Seal the pressure lid, choose Pressure, set to High, and set the timer to 1 minute. Press Start. When ready, release the pressure quickly. Drain the beans and set aside. Rinse and pat dry the inner pot.
2. Return inner pot to pressure cooker, add oil to the pot and press Sear/Sauté. Add onion to the oil and cook for 3 minutes until soft. Add celery and pepper and cook for 1 to 2 minutes until fragrant. Add garlic and cook for 30 seconds until soft; add rice.
3. Transfer the beans back into inner pot and top with broth. Stir black pepper, thyme, cayenne pepper, and salt into mixture. Seal the pressure lid, choose Pressure, set to High, and set the timer to 15 minutes. Press Start.
4. When ready, release pressure quickly. Add more thyme, black pepper and salt as desired.

Southwest Tofu Steaks

Servings: 4
Cooking Time: 30 Minutes
Ingredients:
- Nonstick cooking spray
- 1 pkg. firm tofu, drained & pressed
- 1 tbsp. chili powder
- 1 tsp cumin
- ½ tsp garlic powder
- 1 tsp paprika
- ½ tbsp. oregano
- ½ tbsp. ground coriander
- ½ tsp salt
- 3 tbsp. extra virgin olive oil
- 2 tbsp. water

Directions:
1. Line a baking sheet with foil. Spray fryer basket with cooking spray.
2. Slice tofu in half horizontally. Then slice each half horizontally again.
3. In a small bowl combine remaining ingredients and mix well. Spread mixture over both sides of tofu. Place on prepared pan and let sit 30-45 minutes.
4. Place tofu in fryer basket and add the tender-crisp lid. Set to air fry on 400°F. Cook tofu 30 minutes, turning over halfway through cooking time. Season with salt and pepper and serve immediately.

Nutrition Info:
- InfoCalories 219,Total Fat 18g,Total Carbs 6g,Protein 13g,Sodium 361mg.

Italian Spinach & Tomato Soup

Servings: 6
Cooking Time: 4 Hours
Ingredients:
- 1 tsp olive oil
- 1 onion, chopped
- 3 cloves garlic, chopped fine
- 3 large tomatoes, chopped
- 2 tsp Italian seasoning
- 28 oz. vegetable broth, low sodium
- 10 oz. fresh spinach, trimmed
- ½ tsp pepper
- 2 tbsp. parmesan cheese

Directions:
1. Add the oil to the cooking pot and set to sauté on med-high.
2. Add the onion and garlic and cook, stirring occasionally, 5 minutes or until onion starts to brown.
3. Stir in remaining ingredients, except spinach and parmesan, and mix well. Add the lid and set to slow cook on high. Cook 3-4 hours until tomatoes are tender. Stir occasionally.
4. Add the spinach and cook until it wilts. Ladle into bowls and sprinkle with parmesan. Serve.

Nutrition Info:
- InfoCalories 60,Total Fat 2g,Total Carbs 10g,Protein 3g,Sodium 602mg.

Noodles With Tofu And Peanuts

Servings: 4
Cooking Time: 20 Min
Ingredients:
- 1 package tofu; cubed
- 8 ounces egg noodles /240g
- 2 bell peppers; sliced
- 3 scallions, thinly sliced
- ¼ cup roasted peanuts /32.5g
- ¼ cup soy sauce /62.5ml
- ¼ cup orange juice /62.5ml
- 1 tbsp fresh ginger, peeled and minced /15g
- 2 tbsp vinegar /30ml
- 1 tbsp sesame oil /15ml
- 1 tbsp sriracha /15ml

Directions:
1. In the pressure cooker, mix tofu, bell peppers, orange juice, sesame oil, ginger, egg noodles, soy sauce, vinegar, and sriracha; cover with enough water.
2. Seal the pressure lid, choose Pressure, set to High, and set the timer to 2 minutes. Press Start. When ready, release the pressure quickly. Place the mixture into four plates; apply a topping of scallions and peanuts before serving.

Cheese Crusted Carrot Casserole

Servings: 6
Cooking Time: 40 Minutes
Ingredients:
- 1 ¼ lb. carrots, sliced
- Nonstick cooking spray
- ½ cup light mayonnaise
- ¼ cup onion, chopped fine
- 1 tsp horseradish
- ¼ cup cheddar cheese, reduced fat, grated
- 1 tbsp. whole wheat bread crumbs

Directions:
1. Add the carrots to the cooking pot with enough water to cover them. Set to sauté on high and bring to a boil. Reduce heat to med-low and simmer 7-9 minutes until carrots are tender-crisp. Drain.
2. Spray the cooking pot with cooking spray.
3. In a small bowl, combine mayonnaise, onion, and horseradish, mix well.
4. Return carrots to the cooking pot and spread mayonnaise mixture over the top. Sprinkle the cheese and bread crumbs over the top.
5. Add the tender-crisp lid and set to bake on 350°F. Bake 25-30 minutes until top is golden brown. Serve.

Nutrition Info:
- InfoCalories 121,Total Fat 7g,Total Carbs 12g,Protein 2g,Sodium 245mg.

Leeks And Carrots

Servings: 4
Cooking Time: 15 Minutes
Ingredients:
- 2 leeks, roughly sliced
- 2 carrots, sliced
- 1 teaspoon ginger powder
- 1 teaspoon garlic powder
- ½ cup chicken stock
- Black pepper and salt to the taste
- 2 tablespoons lemon juice
- 2 tablespoons olive oil
- ½ tablespoon balsamic vinegar

Directions:
1. In your Ninja Foodi, combine the leeks with the carrots and the other ingredients.
2. Put the Ninja Foodi's lid on and cook on High for 15 minutes.
3. Release the pressure quickly for 5 minutes, divide the mix between plates and serve.

Nutrition Info:
- InfoCalories: 133; Fat: 3.4g; Carbohydrates: 5g; Protein: 2.1g

Mashed Broccoli With Cream Cheese

Servings: 4
Cooking Time: 12 Min
Ingredients:
- 3 heads broccoli; chopped
- 2 cloves garlic, crushed
- 6 oz. cream cheese /180g
- 2 cups water /500ml
- 2 tbsp butter, unsalted /30g
- Salt and black pepper to taste

Directions:
1. Turn on the Ninja Foodi and select Sear/Sauté mode, adjust to High. Drop in the butter, once it melts add the garlic and cook for 30 seconds while stirring frequently to prevent the garlic from burning.
2. Then, add the broccoli, water, salt, and pepper. Close the lid, secure the pressure valve, and select Pressure mode on High pressure for 5 minutes. Press Start/Stop.
3. Once the timer has ended, do a quick pressure release and use a stick blender to mash the Ingredients until smooth to your desired consistency and well combined.
4. Stir in Cream cheese. Adjust the taste with salt and pepper. Close the crisping lid and cook for 2 minutes on Broil mode. Serve warm.

Pomegranate Radish Mix

Servings: 4
Cooking Time: 8 Minutes
Ingredients:
- 1-pound radishes, roughly cubed
- Black pepper and salt to the taste
- 2 garlic cloves, minced
- ½ cup chicken stock
- 2 tablespoons pomegranate juice
- ¼ cup pomegranate seeds

Directions:
1. In your Ninja Foodi, combine the radishes with the stock and the other ingredients.
2. Put the Ninja Foodi's lid on and cook on High for 8 minutes.
3. Release the pressure quickly for 5 minutes, divide everything between plates and serve.

Nutrition Info:
- InfoCalories: 133; Fat: 2.3g; Carbohydrates: 2.4g; Protein: 2g

Hot & Sour Soup

Servings: 5
Cooking Time: 20 Minutes
Ingredients:
- 3 ½ cups chicken broth, low sodium, divided
- ½ lb. firm tofu, cut in 1-inch cubes
- ¼ lb. mushrooms, sliced
- 3 tbsp. soy sauce, low sodium
- 3 tbsp. vinegar
- 1 tsp ginger
- ½ tsp pepper
- 2 tbsp. cornstarch
- 1 egg, lightly beaten
- ½ cup fresh bean sprouts
- ½ tsp sesame oil

Directions:
1. Add 3 ¼ cups broth, tofu, mushrooms, soy sauce, vinegar, ginger, and pepper to the cooking pot and stir well.
2. Set to sauté on medium heat and bring to a boil.
3. In a small bowl, whisk together remaining broth and cornstarch until smooth. Reduce heat to low and whisk in cornstarch mixture until thickened.
4. Slowly stir in egg to form egg "ribbons". Add bean sprouts and simmer 1-2 minutes or until heated through. Stir in sesame oil and serve immediately.
5. Slowly stir in egg to form egg strands. Add bean sprouts and simmer 1 to 2 minutes, or until heated through, stirring occasionally.

Nutrition Info:
- InfoCalories 123,Total Fat 6g,Total Carbs 8g,Protein 11g,Sodium 978mg.

Roasted Squash And Rice With Crispy Tofu

Servings: 4
Cooking Time: 70 Min
Ingredients:
- 1 small butternut squash, peeled and diced
- 1 block extra-firm tofu, drained and cubed /450g
- 1 cup jasmine rice, cooked /130g
- ¾ cup water /188ml
- 1 tbsp coconut aminos /15g
- 2 tbsps melted butter; divided /30ml
- 2 tsp s arrowroot starch /10g
- 1 tsp salt /5g
- 1 tsp freshly ground black pepper /5g

Directions:
1. Pour the rice and water into the pot and mix with a spoon. Seal the pressure lid, choose Pressure, set to High and set the time to 2 minutes. Choose Start/Stop to boil the rice.
2. in a bowl, toss the butternut squash with 1 tbsp of melted butter and season with the salt and black pepper. Set aside.
3. In another bowl, mix the remaining butter with the coconut aminos, and toss the tofu in the mixture. Pour the arrowroot starch over the tofu and toss again to combine well.
4. When done cooking the rice, perform a quick pressure release, and carefully open the pressure lid. Put the reversible rack in the pot in the higher position and line with aluminum foil. Arrange the tofu and butternut squash on the rack.
5. Close the crisping lid. Choose Air Crisp, set the temperature to 400°F or 205°C, and set the time to 20 minutes. Choose Start/Stop to begin cooking.
6. After 10 minutes, use tongs to turn the butternut squash and tofu. When done cooking, check for your desired crispiness and serve the tofu and squash with the rice.

Veggie And Quinoa Stuffed Peppers

Servings: 1
Cooking Time: 16 Min
Ingredients:
- ¼ cup cooked quinoa /32.5g
- ½ diced tomato, plus one tomato slice
- 1 bell pepper
- ½ tbsp diced onion /7.5g
- 1 tsp olive oil /5ml
- ¼ tsp smoked paprika/1.25g
- ¼ tsp dried basil /1.25g
- Salt and pepper, to taste

Directions:
1. Core and clean the bell pepper to prepare it for stuffing. Brush the pepper with half of the olive oil on the outside.
2. In a small bowl, combine all of the other Ingredients, except the tomato slice and reserved half-tsp olive oil. Stuff the pepper with the filling. Top with the tomato slice.
3. Brush the tomato slice with the remaining half-tsp of oil and sprinkle with basil. Close the crisping lid and cook for 10 minutes on Air Crisp mode at 350 °F or 177°C.

Stuffed Mushrooms

Servings: 4
Cooking Time: 40 Min
Ingredients:
- 10 large white mushrooms, stems removed
- 1 red bell pepper, seeded and chopped
- 1 small onion; chopped
- 1 green onion; chopped
- ¼ cup roasted red bell peppers; chopped /32.5g
- ¼ cup grated Parmesan cheese /32.5g
- ½ cup water/125ml
- 1 tbsp butter /15g
- ½ tsp dried oregano /2.5g
- Salt and black pepper to taste

Directions:
1. Turn on the Ninja Foodi and select Sear/Sauté mode on Medium. Put in the butter to melt and add the roasted and fresh peppers, green onion, onion, oregano, salt, and pepper. Use a spoon to mix and cook for 2 minutes.
2. Spoon the bell pepper mixture into the mushrooms and use a paper towel to wipe the pot and place the stuffed mushrooms in it, 5 at a time. Pour in water.
3. Close the lid, secure the pressure valve, and select pressure mode on High pressure for 5 minutes. Press Start/Stop. Once the timer has ended, do a quick pressure release and open the lid.
4. Sprinkle with parmesan cheese and close the crisping lid. Select Bake/Roast, adjust the temperature to 380°F or 194°C and the time to 2 minutes and press Start/Stop button.
5. Use a set of tongs to remove the stuffed mushrooms onto a plate and repeat the cooking process for the remaining mushrooms. Serve hot with a side of steamed green veggies and a sauce.

Steamed Artichokes With Lemon Aioli

Servings: 4
Cooking Time: 20 Min
Ingredients:
- 4 artichokes, trimmed
- 1 small handful parsley; chopped
- 1 lemon, halved
- 3 cloves garlic, crushed
- ½ cup mayonnaise /125ml
-
- 1 cup water /250ml
- 1 tsp lemon zest /5g
- 1 tbsp lemon juice /15ml
- Salt to taste

Directions:
1. On the artichokes cut ends, rub with lemon. Add water into the pot of pressure cooker. Set the reversible rack over the water,
2. Place the artichokes into the steamer basket with the points upwards; sprinkle each with salt. Seal lid and cook on High pressure for 10 minutes. Press Start. When ready, release the pressure quickly.
3. In a mixing bowl, combine mayonnaise, garlic, lemon juice, and lemon zest. Season to taste with salt. Serve with warm steamed artichokes sprinkled with parsley.

Veggie Potpie

Servings:6
Cooking Time: 22 Minutes
Ingredients:
- Find Ginnie at Hellolittlehome.com
- 4 tablespoons unsalted butter
- ½ large onion, diced
- 1½ cups diced carrot
- 1½ cups diced celery
- 2 garlic cloves, minced
- 3 cups red potatoes, diced
- 1 cup vegetable broth
- ½ cup frozen peas
-
- ½ cup frozen corn
- 1 tablespoon chopped fresh Italian parsley
- 2 teaspoons fresh thyme leaves
- ¼ cup all-purpose flour
- ½ cup heavy (whipping) cream
- Salt
- Freshly ground black pepper
- 1 prepared piecrust

Directions:
1. Select SEAR/SAUTÉ and set temperature to MD:HI. Set the time to 5 minutes to preheat. Select START/STOP to begin.
2. Add the butter to the pot to melt. Add the onion, carrot, and celery to the melted butter. Sauté for about 3 minutes until softened.
3. Stir in the garlic and cook, stirring constantly, for about 30 seconds until fragrant. Select START/STOP to end the function.
4. Add the potatoes and vegetable broth to pot and stir to combine.
5. Assemble the pressure lid, making sure the pressure release valve is in the SEAL position.
6. Select PRESSURE and set to HI. Set the time to 5 minutes. Select START/STOP to begin.
7. When pressure cooking is complete, quick release the pressure by turning the pressure release valve to the VENT position. Carefully remove the lid when the unit has finished releasing pressure.
8. Add the peas, corn, parsley, and thyme to the pot. Season with salt and pepper. Sprinkle the flour over the top and stir to mix well. Stir in the heavy cream.
9. Select SEAR/SAUTÉ and set temperature to MD:HI. Select START/STOP to begin. Cook for 2 to 3 minutes, stirring constantly, until the sauce thickens and is hot. Select START/STOP to end the function.
10. Place the piecrust over the vegetable mixture. Fold over the edges of the crust to fit the pot. Make a small slit in the center of the crust for steam to release. Close the crisping lid.
11. Select BROIL. Set the time to 10 minutes. Select START/STOP to begin.
12. After the cooking is complete, carefully transfer the inner pot to a heat-proof surface. Let the potpie sit for 10 minutes before serving.

Nutrition Info:
- InfoCalories: 361,Total Fat: 22g,Sodium: 339mg,Carbohydrates: 36g,Protein: 6g.

Veggie Primavera

Servings: 6
Cooking Time: 25 Minutes
Ingredients:
- 2 tbsp. olive oil
- 1 tsp Italian seasoning
- 1 tsp garlic powder
- ½ tsp salt
- ½ tsp pepper
- 12 oz. baby red potatoes, quartered
- 2 ears corn, husked & cut into 1-inch rounds
- 4 oz. baby carrots
- ½ red onion, cut in wedges
- 4 oz. fresh sugar snap peas

Directions:
1. In a large bowl, combine oil, Italian seasoning, garlic powder, salt, and pepper, mix well.
2. Add remaining ingredients, except peas, and toss to coat the vegetables.
3. Spray the cooking pot with cooking spray and add the vegetable mixture.
4. Add the tender-crisp lid and set to roast on 425°F. Roast vegetables 15 minutes, turning halfway through cooking time.
5. Add the peas and stir to mix. Roast another 10-15 minutes until vegetables are lightly browned and tender. Serve immediately.

Nutrition Info:
- InfoCalories 142,Total Fat 5g,Total Carbs 23g,Protein 3g,Sodium 222mg.

Maple Dipped Kale

Servings: 4
Cooking Time: 15 Minutes
Ingredients:
- 2 pounds kale, torn
- ½ cup soy sauce
- 1 teaspoon choc zero maple syrup
- 2 teaspoons olive oil
- ½ teaspoon garlic powder
- Black pepper and salt

Directions:
1. In your Ninja Foodi, combine the kale with the soy sauce and the other ingredients.
2. Put the Ninja Foodi's lid on and cook on High for 15 minutes.
3. Release the pressure quickly for 5 minutes, divide everything between plates and serve.

Nutrition Info:
- InfoCalories: 120; Fat: 3.5g; Carbohydrates: 3.3g; Protein: 1.1g

Tomato Galette

Servings: 4
Cooking Time: 40 Minutes

Ingredients:
- ½ pound mixed tomatoes, cut into ¼-inch slices
- 3 inches of leek, thinly sliced
- 2 garlic cloves, diced
- Kosher salt
- 1 store-bought refrigerated pie crust
- 2 tablespoons bread crumbs
- 4 tablespoons shredded Parmesan cheese, divided
- 4 tablespoons shredded mozzarella, divided
- 1 egg, beaten
- Freshly ground black pepper

Directions:
1. Place the tomatoes, leeks, and garlic into large bowl. Sprinkle with salt and set aside for at least 5 minutes to draw out the juices from the vegetables.
2. Strain the excess juice off the tomato mixture and pat down the vegetables with paper towels.
3. Unroll the pie crust and place it in the Ninja Multi-Purpose Pan or a 1½-quart round ceramic baking dish and form it to the bottom of the pan. Lay the extra dough loosely on the sides of the pan.
4. Sprinkle the bread crumbs in a thin layer on the pie crust bottom, then scatter 3 tablespoons each of Parmesan and mozzarella cheese on top. Place the tomato mixture in a heap in the middle of the dough and top with the remaining 1 tablespoon each of Parmesan and mozzarella cheese.
5. Fold the edges of the crust over the tomatoes and brush with the egg.
6. Close crisping lid. Select BAKE/ROAST, set temperature to 350°F, and set time to 45 minutes. Select START/STOP to begin. Let preheat for 5 minutes.
7. Place pan on the Reversible Rack, making sure the rack is in the lower position. Cover galette loosely with aluminum foil (do not seal the pan).
8. Once unit has preheated, open lid and carefully place the rack with pan in the pot. Close crisping lid.
9. After 20 minutes, open lid and remove the foil. Close lid and continue cooking.
10. When cooking is complete, remove rack with pan and set aside to let cool. Cut into slices, season with pepper, and serve.

Nutrition Info:
- InfoCalories: 288, Total Fat: 15g, Sodium: 409mg, Carbohydrates: 31g, Protein: 9g.

Green Squash Gruyere

Servings: 4
Cooking Time: 70 Min

Ingredients:
- 1 large green squash; sliced
- 2 cups tomato sauce /500ml
- 1 cup shredded mozzarella cheese /130g
- 1½ cups panko breadcrumbs /195g
- ⅓ cup grated Gruyere cheese /44g
- 3 tbsps melted unsalted butter /45ml
- 2 tsp s salt /10g

Directions:
1. Season the squash slices on both sides with salt and place the slices on a wire rack to drain liquid for 5 to 10 minutes. In a bowl, combine the melted butter, breadcrumbs, and Gruyere cheese and set aside.
2. Rinse the squash slices with water and blot dry with paper towel. After, arrange the squash in the inner pot in a single layer as much as possible and pour the tomato sauce over the slices.
3. Seal the pressure lid, choose Pressure, set to High, and the time to 5 minutes. Press Start to commence cooking. When the timer has read to the end, perform a quick pressure release. Sprinkle the squash slices with the mozzarella cheese.
4. Close the crisping lid. Choose Bake/Roast; adjust the temperature to 375°F or 191°C and the cook time to 2 minutes. Press Start to broil.
5. After, carefully open the lid and sprinkle the squash with the breadcrumb mixture. Close the crisping lid again, choose Bake/Roast, adjust the temperature to 375°F, and the cook time to 8 minutes. Press Start to continue broiling. Serve immediately.

Cheese And Mushroom Tarts

Servings: 4
Cooking Time: 75 Min

Ingredients:

- 1 small white onion; sliced
- 1 sheet puff pastry, thawed
- 5 ounces oyster mushrooms; sliced /150g
- 1 cup shredded Swiss cheese /130g
- ¼ cup dry white wine /62.5ml
- 1 tbsp thinly sliced fresh green onions /15ml
- 2 tbsps melted butter; divided /30ml
- ¼ tsp salt /1.25g
- ¼ tsp freshly ground black pepper /1.25g

Directions:

1. Choose Sear/Sauté, set to High, and set the time to 5 minutes. Choose Start/Stop to preheat the pot. Add 1 tbsp of butter, the onion, and mushrooms to the pot. Sauté for 5 minutes or until the vegetables are tender and browned.
2. Season with salt and black pepper, pour in the white wine, and cook until evaporated, about 2 minutes. Spoon the vegetables into a bowl and set aside.
3. Unwrap the puff pastry and cut into 4 squares. Pierce the dough with a fork and brush both sides with the remaining oil. Share half of the cheese evenly over the puff pastry squares, leaving a ½- inch border around the edges. Also, share the mushroom mixture over the pastry squares and top with the remaining cheese.
4. Put the Crisping Basket in the pot. Close the crisping lid, choose Air Crisp, set the temperature to 400°F, and the time to 5 minutes.
5. Once the pot has preheated, put 1 tart in the Crisping Basket. Close the crisping lid, choose Air Crisp, set the temperature to 360°F or 183°C, and set the time to 6 minutes; press Start.
6. After 6 minutes, check the tart for your preferred brownness. Take the tart out of the basket and transfer to a plate. Repeat the process with the remaining tarts. Garnish with the green onions and serve.

Cauliflower Enchiladas

Servings: 5
Cooking Time: 25 Minutes

Ingredients:

- 2 tablespoons canola oil
- 1 large head cauliflower, cut into 1-inch florets
- 2 teaspoons ground cumin
- 1 teaspoon ground chili pepper
- 2 teaspoons kosher salt
- ½ teaspoon freshly ground black pepper
- 1 can diced tomatoes, drained
- 5 flour tortillas
- 1 can red enchilada sauce
- 1½ cups shredded Mexican blend cheese
- ½ cup chopped cilantro, for garnish

Directions:

1. In a medium bowl, toss together the oil, cauliflower, cumin, chili pepper, salt, and black pepper. Place the cauliflower in the Cook & Crisp Basket and place the basket in pot. Close crisping lid.
2. Select AIR CRISP, set temperature to 390°F, and set time to 15 minutes. Select START/STOP to begin.
3. After 8 minutes, open lid, then lift the basket and shake the cauliflower. Lower basket back into pot and close lid. Continue cooking, until the cauliflower reaches your desired crispiness.
4. When cooking is complete, remove basket from pot. Place the cauliflower in a bowl and mix with the tomatoes.
5. Lay the tortillas on a work surface. Divide the cauliflower-
6. tomato mixture between the tortillas and roll them up. Place the filled tortillas seam-side down in the pot. Pour the enchilada sauce on top.
7. Close crisping lid. Select BROIL and set time to 10 minutes. Select START/STOP to begin.
8. After 5 minutes, open lid and add the cheese on top. Close lid and continue cooking until cheese is golden brown.
9. When cooking is complete, add cilantro and serve.

Nutrition Info:

- InfoCalories: 315,Total Fat: 19g,Sodium: 822mg,Carbohydrates: 28g,Protein: 13g.

Whole Roasted Cabbage With White Wine Cream Sauce

Servings: 8
Cooking Time: 32 Minutes
Ingredients:
- 1 head green cabbage
- ½ cup, plus 1 tablespoon water
- 1 tablespoon extra-virgin olive oil
- Kosher salt
- Freshly ground black pepper
- 2 cups white wine
- ¼ cup minced red onion
- 1 cup heavy (whipping) cream
- ¼ cup minced fresh dill
- ¼ cup minced fresh parsley
- 2 tablespoons whole-grain mustard
- 1 tablespoon cornstarch

Directions:
1. Place the cabbage and ½ cup of water, stem-side down, in the pot.
2. With a knife cut an X into the top of the cabbage cutting all the way through to the bottom through the core. Assemble pressure lid, making sure the pressure release valve is in the SEAL position.
3. Select PRESSURE and set temperature to HI. Set time to 15 minutes. Select START/STOP to begin.
4. When pressure cooking is complete, quick release the pressure by turning the pressure release valve to the VENT position. Carefully remove lid when unit has finished releasing pressure.
5. Brush the cabbage with the olive oil and season with salt and pepper. Close crisping lid.
6. Select AIR CRISP, set temperature to 390°F, and set time to 12 minutes. Select START/STOP to begin.
7. Once cooking is complete, open lid, lift out the cabbage, wrap with foil, and set aside. Leave any remaining water in the pot.
8. Select SEAR/SAUTÉ. Set temperature to HI. Select START/STOP to begin.
9. Add the white wine and onion and stir, scraping any brown bits off the bottom of the pot. Stir in the cream, dill, parsley, and mustard. Let simmer for 5 minutes.
10. In a small bowl, whisk together the cornstarch and the remaining 1 tablespoon of water until smooth. Stir it into the mixture in the pot. Cook until the sauce has thickened and coats the back of a spoon, about 2 minutes.
11. Pour half of the sauce over the cabbage. Cut the cabbage into 8 pieces and serve with remaining sauce.

Nutrition Info:
- InfoCalories: 206,Total Fat: 14g,Sodium: 129mg,Carbohydrates: 10g,Protein: 3g.

Cheesy Chilies

Servings: 4
Cooking Time: 25 Minutes
Ingredients:
- Nonstick cooking spray
- 2 poblano chilies, halved, seeded, stems on
- 1 cup cottage cheese, drained
- ¼ cup green onion, chopped
- ½ cup Colby-Jack cheese, grated

Directions:
1. Spray the fryer basket with cooking spray.
2. Place the chilies in the basket and add the tender-crisp lid. Set to broil. Cook chilies until skin is charred on all sides. Transfer to a bag and let cool. When cool, remove the skin.
3. Spray an 8x8-inch baking pan with cooking spray.
4. Place chilies in the prepared pan. Spoon cottage cheese in the chilies and sprinkle with green onion and Colby Jack cheese.
5. Place the rack in the cooking pot and add the baking pan. Add the tender-crisp lid and set to bake on 350°F. Bake 15-20 minutes until hot and cheese is melted. Serve immediately.

Nutrition Info:
- InfoCalories 119,Total Fat 7g,Total Carbs 5g,Protein 10g,Sodium 313mg.

Cheesy Spicy Pasta

Servings: 6
Cooking Time: 40 Minutes
Ingredients:
- 1 ½ cups cottage cheese, low fat
- ½ cup ricotta cheese
- ½ cup Greek yogurt
- 2 cups mozzarella cheese, grated, divided
- ¼ cup fresh parsley, chopped
- 2 cups baby spinach
- 1 tbsp. butter
- 1 onion, chopped
- 2 tbsp. garlic, chopped fine
- 14 ½ oz. fire-roasted tomatoes
- 8 oz. tomato sauce
- ½ tsp red pepper flakes
- 1 ½ tsp oregano
- 1 tsp rosemary
- ½ tsp salt
- ½ tsp pepper
- ¾ lb. whole grain pasta, cooked & drained
- 6 tbsp. parmesan cheese

Directions:
1. In a medium bowl, combine cottage cheese, ricotta, yogurt, 1 cup mozzarella, parsley, and spinach, mix well.
2. Add the butter to the cooking pot and set to sauté on med-high. Once the butter melts, add the onion and cook until translucent. Add the garlic and cook 1 minute more.
3. Stir in tomatoes, tomato sauce, and seasonings, reduce heat to low and simmer 5 minutes.
4. Stir in the pasta and the ricotta mixture, mix well. Top with remaining mozzarella and the parmesan cheese.
5. Add the tender-crisp lid and set to bake on 400°F. Bake 25-30 minutes until hot and bubbly. Serve.

Nutrition Info:
- InfoCalories 282,Total Fat 7g,Total Carbs 30g,Protein 28g,Sodium 522mg.

Grilled Tofu Sandwich

Servings: 1
Cooking Time: 20 Min
Ingredients:
- 2 slices of bread
- ¼ cup red cabbage, shredded /32.5g
- 1-inch thick Tofu slice
- 2 tsp olive oil divided /10ml
- ¼ tsp vinegar /1.25ml
- Salt and pepper, to taste

Directions:
1. Place the bread slices and toast for 3 minutes on Roast mode at 350 F; set aside. Brush the tofu with 1 tsp of oil, and place in the basket of the Ninja Foodi. Bake for 5 minutes on each side on Roast mode at 350 °F or 177°C.
2. Combine the cabbage, remaining oil, and vinegar, and season with salt and pepper.
3. Place the tofu on top of one bread slice, place the cabbage over, and top with the other bread slice.

Desserts

Créme Brulee

Servings: 4
Cooking Time: 30 Min + 6 Hours Of Cooling
Ingredients:
- 3 cups heavy whipping cream /750ml
- 7 large egg yolks
- 2 cups water /500mll
- 6 tbsp sugar /90g
- 2 tbsp vanilla extract /30ml

Directions:
1. In a mixing bowl, add the yolks, vanilla, whipping cream, and half of the swerve sugar. Use a whisk to mix them until they are well combined. Pour the mixture into the ramekins and cover them with aluminium foil.
2. Open the Foodi, fit the reversible rack into the pot, and pour in the water.
3. Place 3 ramekins on the rack and place the remaining ramekins to sit on the edges of the ramekins below.
4. Close the lid, secure the pressure valve, and select Pressure mode on High for 8 minutes. Press Start/Stop.
5. Once the timer has stopped, do a natural pressure release for 10 minutes, then a quick pressure release to let out the remaining pressure.
6. With a napkin in hand, remove the ramekins onto a flat surface and then into a refrigerator to chill for at least 6 hours. After refrigeration, remove the ramekins and remove the aluminium foil.
7. Equally, sprinkle the remaining sugar on it and return to the pot. Close the crisping lid, select Bake/Roast mode, set the timer to 4 minutes on 380 °F or 194°C. Serve the crème brulee chilled with whipped cream.

Coconut Cream "custard" Bars

Servings:8
Cooking Time: 20 Minutes
Ingredients:
- 1¼ cups all-purpose flour
- 6 tablespoons unsalted butter, melted
- 2 tablespoons granulated sugar
- ½ cup unsweetened shredded coconut, divided
- ½ cup chopped almonds, divided
- Cooking spray
- 1 package instant vanilla pudding
- 1 cup milk
- 1 cup heavy (whipping) cream
- 4 tablespoons finely chopped dark chocolate, divided

Directions:
1. Select BAKE/ROAST, set temperature to 375°F, and set time to 15 minutes. Select START/STOP to begin. Let preheat for 5 minutes.
2. To make the crust, combine the flour, butter, sugar, ¼ cup of coconut, and ¼ cup of almonds in a large bowl and stir until a crumbly dough forms.
3. Grease the Ninja Multi-Purpose Pan or an 8-inch round baking dish with cooking spray. Place the dough in the pan and press it into an even layer covering the bottom.
4. Once unit has preheated, place pan on Reversible Rack, making sure the rack is in the lower position. Open lid and place rack in pot. Close crisping lid. Reduce temperature to 325°F.
5. Place remaining ¼ cup each of almonds and coconut in a Ninja Loaf Pan or any small loaf pan and set aside.
6. When cooking is complete, remove rack with pan and let cool for 10 minutes.
7. Quickly place the loaf pan with coconut and almonds in the bottom of the pot. Close crisping lid.
8. Select AIR CRISP, set temperature to 350°F, and set time to 10 minutes. Select START/STOP to begin.
9. While the nuts and coconut toast, whisk together the instant pudding with the milk, cream, and 3 tablespoons of chocolate.
10. After 5 minutes, open lid and stir the coconut and almonds. Close lid and continue cooking for another 5 minutes.
11. When cooking is complete, open lid and remove pan from pot. Add the almonds and coconut to the pudding. Stir until fully incorporated. Pour this in a smooth, even layer on top of the crust.
12. Refrigerate for about 10 minutes. Garnish with the remaining 1 tablespoon of chocolate, cut into wedges, and serve.

Nutrition Info:
- InfoCalories: 476,Total Fat: 33g,Sodium: 215mg,Carbohydrates: 39g,Protein: 6g.

Churro Bites

Servings: 7
Cooking Time: 12 Minutes

Ingredients:
- Cooking spray
- 1 box cinnamon swirl crumb cake and muffin mix, brown sugar mix packet removed and reserved
- 2 large eggs
- 1 cup buttermilk
- 1 teaspoon ground cinnamon, divided
- ¼ cup packed light brown sugar
- 1½ cups water
- 1 tablespoon granulated sugar
- Chocolate sauce, for serving (optional)
- Caramel sauce, for serving (optional)
- Strawberry sauce, for serving (optional)
- Whipped topping, for serving (optional)
- Peanut butter, for serving (optional)

Directions:
1. Lightly coat 2 egg bite molds with cooking spray and set aside.
2. In a large bowl, combine the cake mix, brown sugar mix packet, eggs, buttermilk, and ½ teaspoon of cinnamon. Mix until evenly combined.
3. Using a cookie scoop, transfer the batter to the prepared mold, filling each three-quarters full. Tightly cover the molds with aluminum foil, or with the silicone cover that came with the egg molds.
4. Pour the water into the cooking pot. Place the egg molds onto the Reversible Rack in the lower steam position and lower into the pot.
5. If using a foil sling (see TIP), ensure the foil cover is tight enough to support the egg mold that will sit on top. Rotate the top egg mold slightly to ensure that the molds do not press into one another.
6. Assemble the pressure lid, making sure the pressure release valve is in the SEAL position.
7. Select PRESSURE and set to HI. Set the time to 12 minutes. Select START/STOP to begin.
8. When pressure cooking is complete, allow the pressure to naturally release for 10 minutes. After 10 minutes, quick release any remaining pressure by moving the pressure release valve to the VENT position. Carefully remove the lid when the unit has finished releasing pressure.
9. In a small bowl, stir together the brown sugar, granulated sugar, and remaining ½ teaspoon of cinnamon. Set aside.
10. Using the sling, remove the egg molds from the pot and let cool for 5 minutes.
11. One at a time, place a plate over the egg mold and flip the mold over. Gently press on the mold to release the churro bites.
12. Roll the warm churro bites in the brown sugar mixture, and sprinkle any remaining brown sugar on top. Serve with your favorite dipping sauce.

Nutrition Info:
- Info.

Raspberry Cheesecake

Servings: 6
Cooking Time: 30 Min
Ingredients:
- 1 ½ cups Graham Cracker Crust /195g
- ¾ cup Sugar /98g
- 1 cup Raspberries /130g
- 1 ½ cups Water /375ml
- 3 cups Cream Cheese /390g
- 3 Eggs
- ½ stick Butter, melted
- 1 tbsp fresh Orange Juice /15ml
- 1 tsp Vanilla Paste /5g
- 1 tsp finely grated Orange Zest /5g

Directions:
1. Insert the reversible rack into the Foodi, and add 1 ½ cups or 375ml of water. Grease a spring form. Mix in graham cracker crust with sugar and butter, in a bowl. Press the mixture to form a crust at the bottom.
2. Blend the raspberries and cream cheese with an electric mixer. Crack in the eggs and keep mixing until well combined. Mix in the remaining ingredients, and give it a good stir.
3. Pour this mixture into the pan, and cover the pan with aluminium foil. Lay the spring form on the tray. Select Pressure and set the time to 20 minutes at High pressure. Press Start. Once the cooking is complete, do a quick pressure release. Refrigerate the cheesecake for at least 2 hours.

Sweet And Salty Bars

Servings:12
Cooking Time: 10 Minutes
Ingredients:
- 1 cup light corn syrup
- 1 cup granulated sugar
- 1 teaspoon vanilla extract
- 1 bag mini marshmallows
- 1 cup crunchy peanut butter
- 1 bag potato chips with ridges, slightly crushed
- 1 cup pretzels, slightly crushed
- 1 bag hard-shelled candy-coated chocolates

Directions:
1. Select SEAR/SAUTÉ and set temperature to MD:HI. Select START/STOP to begin. Let preheat for 5 minutes.
2. Add the corn syrup, sugar, and vanilla and stir until the sugar is melted.
3. Add the marshmallows and peanut butter and stir until the marshmallows are melted.
4. Add the potato chips and pretzels and stir until everything is evenly coated in the marshmallow mixture.
5. Pour the mixture into a 9-by-13-inch pan and place the chocolate candies on top, slightly pressing them in. Let cool, then cut into squares and serve.

Nutrition Info:
- InfoCalories: 585,Total Fat: 21g,Sodium: 403mg,Carbohydrates: 96g,Protein: 9g.

Cheat Apple Pie

Servings: 9
Cooking Time: 30 Min
Ingredients:
- 4 apples; diced
- 1 egg, beaten
- 3 large puff pastry sheets
- 2 oz. sugar /60g
- 1 oz. brown sugar /30g
- 2 oz. butter, melted /60ml
- 2 tsp cinnamon /10g
- ¼ tsp salt /1.25g

Directions:
1. Whisk the white sugar, brown sugar, cinnamon, salt, and butter together. Place the apples in a baking dish and coat them with the mixture.
2. Slide the dish into the Foodi and cook for 10 minutes on Roast at 350 °F or 177°C.
3. Meanwhile, roll out the pastry on a floured flat surface, and cut each sheet into 6 equal pieces. Divide the apple filling between the parts.
4. Brush the edges of the pastry squares with the egg. Fold and seal the edges with a fork. Place on a lined baking sheet and cook in the fryer at 350 °F or 177°C for 8 minutes on Roast. Flip over, increase the temperature to 390 °F or 177°C, and cook for 2 more minutes.

Irish Cream Flan

Servings: 3
Cooking Time: 10 Minutes
Ingredients:
- ¼ cup + 2 tbsp. sugar, divided
- 1 tbsp. water
- 1 cup half and half
- ¼ cup Irish cream flavored coffee creamer
- ¼ cup Irish cream liqueur
- 2 eggs

Directions:
1. In a small saucepan over medium heat, heat ¼ cup sugar until melted and a deep amber color. Swirl the pan occasionally to distribute the heat.
2. When the sugar reaches the right color remove from heat and carefully stir in the water until combined. Drizzle over the bottoms of 3 ramekins.
3. In a small oven-safe bowl, whisk the eggs.
4. In a small saucepan over medium heat, stir together half and half, creamer, Irish cream, and remaining sugar. Heat to simmering.
5. Gradually whisk the warm liquids into the eggs 2 tablespoons at a time, whisking constantly. After a 1/3 of the cream mixture has been added, slowly pour the remaining mixture into the eggs, whisking constantly until combined.
6. Pour 1 cup water into the cooking pot and add the trivet.
7. Pour the egg mixture into the ramekins and cover tightly with foil. Place them on the trivet.
8. Secure the lid and set to pressure cooking on high. Set the timer for 5 minutes. When the timer goes off, use natural release to remove the lid. Transfer custards to a wire rack and uncover to cool.
9. Cover with plastic wrap and refrigerate at least 4 hours before serving. To serve, use a small knife to loosen the custards from the sides of the ramekin and invert onto serving plate.

Nutrition Info:
- InfoCalories 215,Total Fat 9g,Total Carbs 25g,Protein 7g,Sodium 134mg.

Coffee Cake

Servings: 8
Cooking Time: 30 Minutes
Ingredients:

- Cooking spray
- 1 box yellow cake mix
- 1 cup water
- ⅓ cup vegetable oil
- 3 large eggs
-
- 4 cups all-purpose flour
- 1 cup granulated sugar
- 3 tablespoons cinnamon
- 2 cups unsalted butter, melted
- Confectioners' sugar, for garnish

Directions:
1. Grease a Ninja Tube Pan or a 7-inch Bundt pan with cooking spray.
2. Close crisping lid. Select BAKE/ROAST, set temperature to 325°F, and set time to 5 minutes. Select START/STOP to begin preheating.
3. In a large bowl, mix together the cake mix, water, oil, and eggs until combined. Pour the batter into the prepared pan.
4. When unit has preheated, place pan on Reversible Rack, making sure the rack is in the lower position. Open lid and place rack with pan in pot. Close crisping lid.
5. Select BAKE/ROAST, set temperature to 325°F, and set time to 30 minutes. Select START/STOP to begin.
6. In another large bowl, combine the flour, sugar, and cinnamon. Add the butter and mix until well combined and the mixture is a crumble.
7. After 25 minutes, open lid and check for doneness. If a toothpick inserted into the cake comes out clean, the cake is done. If necessary, close lid and continue baking.
8. Open lid and spread the crumble topping on top of the cakes. Close lid and bake for an additional 4 to 5 minutes.
9. When cooking is complete, carefully remove pan from pot and place it on a cooling rack. Let cool. Using a fine mesh sieve, garnish the coffee cake with confectioners' sugar.

Nutrition Info:
- InfoCalories: 1152,Total Fat: 65g,Sodium: 464mg,Carbohydrates: 132g,Protein: 13g.

Chocolate Walnut Cake

Servings: 6
Cooking Time: 20 Minutes
Ingredients:

- 3 eggs
- 1 cup almond flour
- 2/3 cup Erythritol
- 1/3 cup heavy whipping cream
-
- ¼ cup butter softened
- ¼ cup cacao powder
- ¼ cup walnuts, chopped
- 1 teaspoon baking powder

Directions:
1. In a suitable bowl, mix all the ingredients and with a mixer, beat until fluffy.
2. Add the mixture into a greased Bundt pan.
3. With a piece of foil, cover the pan.
4. In the Ninja Foodi's insert, place 2 cups of water.
5. Set a "Reversible Rack" in the Ninja Foodi's insert.
6. Place the Bundt pan over the "Reversible Rack".
7. Close the Ninja Foodi's lid with a pressure lid and place the pressure valve to the "Seal" position.
8. Select "Pressure" mode and set it to "High" for 20 minutes.
9. Press the "Start/Stop" button to initiate cooking.
10. Switch the pressure valve to "Vent" and do a "Quick" release.
11. Place the pan onto a wire rack to cool for about 10 minutes.
12. Flip the baked and cooled cake onto the wire rack to cool completely.
13. Cut into desired-sized slices and serve.

Nutrition Info:
- InfoCalories: 270; Fats: 25.4g; Carbohydrates: 7g; Proteins: 8.9g

Chocolate Bread Pudding With Caramel Sauce

Servings: 14
Cooking Time: 3 Hours
Ingredients:
- Butter flavored cooking spray
- 8 cups whole wheat bread, cubed
- 1 cup dark chocolate chips
- ¼ cup cocoa powder, unsweetened
- ½ cup + 1/3 cup Stevia
- 1 cup pecans, chopped, divided
- 1/8 tsp salt
- 2 eggs
- 4 egg whites
- 1 2/3 cup skim milk, divided
- 1 cup almond milk, unsweetened
- 3 tsp vanilla, divided
- 1 tbsp. cornstarch

Directions:
1. Spray cooking pot with cooking spray. Add the bread cubes.
2. In a medium bowl, combine chocolate chips, cocoa, ½ cup Stevia, ¾ cup nuts, and salt, mix well.
3. Whisk in eggs, egg whites, 1 cup milk, coconut milk, and 1 teaspoon vanilla until smooth. Pour over bread and stir to make sure all of the bread cubes are covered. Sprinkle remaining nuts over the top.
4. Add the lid and set to slow cooking on low. Cook 3 hours or until bread pudding passes the toothpick test.
5. In a medium saucepan, combine remaining Stevia and cornstarch. Stir in remaining milk and cook over med-low heat until sauce has thickened.
6. Remove from heat and stir in remaining 2 teaspoons vanilla. Drizzle over bread pudding and serve.

Nutrition Info:
- InfoCalories 269,Total Fat 14g,Total Carbs 27g,Protein 8g,Sodium 60mg.

Mini Chocolate Cheesecakes

Servings: 4
Cooking Time: 18 Minutes
Ingredients:
- 1 egg
- 8 ounces cream cheese, softened
- ¼ cup Erythritol
- 1 tablespoon powdered peanut butter
- ¾ tablespoon cacao powder

Directions:
1. Grease the Ninja Foodi's insert.
2. In a blender, stir in the eggs and cream cheese and pulse until smooth.
3. Add the rest of the ingredients and pulse until well combined.
4. Transfer the mixture into 2 8-ounce mason jars evenly.
5. In the Ninja Foodi's insert, place 1 cup of water.
6. Set a "Reversible Rack" in the Ninja Foodi's insert.
7. Place the mason jars over the "Reversible Rack".
8. Close the Ninja Foodi's lid with a pressure lid and place the pressure valve in the "Seal" position.
9. Select "Pressure" mode and set it to "High" for 18 minutes.
10. Press the "Start/Stop" button to initiate cooking.
11. Switch the pressure valve to "Vent" and do a "Natural" release.
12. Open the Ninja Foodi's lid and place the ramekins onto a wire rack to cool.
13. Refrigerate to chill for at least 6-8 hours before serving.

Nutrition Info:
- InfoCalories: 222; Fats: 28.4g; Carbohydrates: 2.9g; Proteins: 6.5g

Vanilla Cheesecake

Servings: 6
Cooking Time: 60 Min
Ingredients:
- 16 ounces cream cheese, at room temperature /480g
- 2 eggs
- ¼ cup sour cream /62.5ml
- 1½ cups finely crushed graham crackers /195g
- 1 cup water /250ml
- ½ cup brown sugar /65g
- 2 tbsps sugar /30g
- 1 tbsp all-purpose flour /15g
- 4 tbsps unsalted butter, melted /60ml
- 1½ tsp s vanilla extract /7.5ml
- ½ tsp salt /2.5ml
- Cooking spray

Directions:
1. Grease a spring form pan with cooking spray, then line the pan with parchment paper, grease with cooking spray again, and line with aluminium foil. This is to ensure that there are no air gaps in the pan. In a medium mixing bowl, mix the graham cracker crumbs, sugar, and butter. Spoon the mixture into the pan and press firmly into with a spoon.
2. In a deep bowl and with a hand mixer, beat the beat the cream cheese and brown sugar until well-mixed. Whisk in the sour cream to be smooth and stir in the flour, vanilla, and salt.
3. Crack the eggs in and beat but not to be overly smooth. Pour the mixture into the pan over the crumbs. Next, pour the water into the pot. Put the spring form pan on the reversible rack and put the rack in the lower positon of the pot.
4. Seal the pressure lid, choose Pressure, set to High, and set the time to 35 minutes. Choose Start/Stop to begin. Once done baking, perform a natural pressure release for 10 minutes, then a quick pressure release to let out any remaining pressure. Carefully open the lid.
5. Remove the pan from the rack and allow the cheesecake to cool for 1 hour. Cover the cheesecake with foil and chill in the refrigerator for 4 hours.

Spiced Poached Pears

Servings: 4
Cooking Time: 4 Hours
Ingredients:
- 4 ripe pears, peeled
- 2 cups fresh orange juice
- ¼ cup maple syrup
- 5 cardamom pods
- 1 cinnamon stick, broke in 2
- 1-inch piece ginger, peeled & sliced

Directions:
1. Slice off the bottom of the pears so they stand upright. Carefully remove the core with a paring knife. Stand in the cooking pot.
2. In a small bowl, whisk together orange juice and syrup. Pour over pears and add the spices.
3. Add the lid and set to slow cooking on low. Cook 3-4 hours or until pears are soft. Baste the pears every hour or so.
4. Serve garnished with whipped cream and chopped walnuts if you like, or just serve them as they are sprinkled with a little cinnamon.

Nutrition Info:
- InfoCalories 219,Total Fat 1g,Total Carbs 53g,Protein 2g,Sodium 6mg.

Dark Chocolate Brownies

Servings: 6
Cooking Time: 40 Min
Ingredients:
- 1 cup water /250ml
- 2 eggs
- ¼ cup olive oil /62.5ml
- ⅓ cup flour /44g
- ⅓ cup cocoa powder /44g
- ⅓ cup dark chocolate chips /44g
- ⅓ cup chopped Walnuts /44g
- ⅓ cup granulated sugar /44g
- 1 tbsp vanilla extract /15ml
- 1 tbsp milk/15ml
- ½ tsp baking powder /2.5g
- A pinch salt

Directions:
1. In the Foodi, add water and set in the reversible rack. Line a parchment paper on. a springform pan. In a bowl, beat eggs and sugar to mix until smooth; stir in olive oil, cocoa powder, milk, salt baking powder, chocolate chips, flour, walnuts, vanilla, and sea salt.
2. Transfer the batter to the prepared springform pan and place the pan in the pot on the rack. Close the crisping lid and select Bake/Roast; adjust the temperature to 250°F or 122°C and the cook time to 20 minutes. Press Start.
3. When the time is up, open the lid and. and allow the brownie to cool for 10 minutes before cutting. Use powdered sugar to dust the brownies before serving lightly.

Apricots With Honey Sauce

Servings: 4
Cooking Time: 15 Min
Ingredients:
- 8 Apricots, pitted and halved
- ¼ cup Honey /62.5ml
- 2 cups Blueberries /260g
- ½ Cinnamon stick
- 1 ¼ cups Water /312.5ml
- ½ Vanilla Bean; sliced lengthwise
- 1 ½ tbsp Cornstarch /22.5g
- ¼ tsp ground Cardamom /1.25g

Directions:
1. Add all ingredients, except for the honey and the cornstarch, to your Foodi. Seal the pressure lid, choose Pressure, set to High, and set the time to s 8 minutes. Press Start. Do a quick pressure release and open the pressure lid.
2. Remove the apricots with a slotted spoon. Choose Sear/Sauté, add the honey and cornstarch, then let simmer until the sauce thickens, for about 5 minutes. Split up the apricots among serving plates and top with the blueberry sauce, to serve.

Caramel Walnut Brownies

Servings: 4
Cooking Time: 60 Min+ Cooling Time
Ingredients:
- 2 large eggs, at room temperature
- 8 ounces white chocolate /240g
- 1 cup sugar /130g
- ½ cup caramel sauce/125ml
- ½ cup toasted walnuts /65g
- ¾ cup all-purpose flour /98g
- 8 tbsps unsalted butter /120g
- 2 tsp s almond extract /10ml
- A pinch of salt
- Cooking spray

Directions:
1. Put the white chocolate and butter in a small bowl and pour 1 cup or 250ml of water into the inner pot. Place the reversible rack in the lower position of the pot and put the bowl on top.
2. Close the crisping lid. Choose Bake/Roast; adjust the temperature to 375°F or 191°C and the cook time to 10 minutes to melt the white chocolate and butter. Press Start. Check after 5 minutes and stir. As soon as the chocolate has melted, remove the bowl from the pot.
3. Use a small spatula to transfer the chocolate mixture into a medium and stir in the almond extract, sugar, and salt. One after another, crack each egg into the bowl and whisk after each addition. Mix in the flour until smooth, about 1 minute.
4. Grease a round cake pan with cooking spray or line the pan with parchment paper. Pour the batter into the prepared pan and place on the rack.
5. Close the crisping lid and Choose Bake/Roast; adjust the temperature to 250°F or 122°C and the cook time to 25 minutes. Press Start. Once the time is up, open the lid and check the brownies. The top should be just set. Blot out the butter that may pool to the top using a paper towel.
6. Close the crisping lid again and adjust the temperature to 300°F or 149°C and the cook time to 15 minutes. Press Start. Once the time is up, open the lid and check the brownies. A toothpick inserted into the center should come out with crumbs sticking to it but no raw batter.
7. Generously drizzle the caramel sauce on top of the brownies and scatter the walnuts on top. Close the crisping lid again and adjust the temperature to 325°F or 163°C and the cook time to 8 minutes; press Start.
8. When the nuts are brown and the caramel is bubbling, take out the brownies, and allow cooling for at least 30 minutes and cut into squares.

Cherry Pie

Servings: 6
Cooking Time: 45 Min
Ingredients:
- 1 9-inch double Pie Crust
- 4 cups Cherries, pitted /520g
- 1 cup Sugar /130g
- 2 cups Water /500ml
- 4 tbsp Quick Tapioca /60g
- ½ tsp Vanilla Extract /2.5ml
- ¼ tsp Almond Extract /1.25ml
- A pinch of Salt

Directions:
1. Pour water inside your cooker and add the reversible rack. Combine the cherries with tapioca, sugar, extracts, and salt, in a bowl. Place one pie crust at the bottom of a lined springform pan.
2. Spread the cherries mixture and top with the other crust. Lower the pan onto the reversible rack.
3. Seal the pressure lid, choose Pressure, set to High, and set the time to 18 minutes. Press Start. Once cooking is completed, do a quick pressure release. Let cool the pie on a cooling rack. Slice to serve.

Moon Milk

Servings: 2
Cooking Time: 10 Min

Ingredients:
- 1/4 cup hemp hearts /32.5g
- 1 cup milk /250ml
- 1 pinch ground nutmeg
- 1 pinch ground ginger
- 1 pinch freshly ground black pepper
- ½ tsp maca powder /2.5g
- 1/8 tsp ground cardamom/0.625g
- ½ tsp ground cinnamon, plus more for garnish /2.5g
- 1 tsp coconut oil /5ml
- ½ tsp ground turmeric /2.5g
- 1 tsp honey /5ml

Directions:
1. To the Foodi, add milk. Press Sear/Sauté and heat the milk for 3-4 minutes until the point of starting to bubble; stir in coconut oil, turmeric, nutmeg, pepper, ginger, hemp hearts, maca powder, cinnamon, and cardamom.
2. Press Start/Stop and allow mixture to cool for about a minute; whisk in honey. Transfer the mixture into a mug. Add more cinnamon for garnishing!

Portuguese Honey Cake

Servings: 8
Cooking Time: 15 Minutes

Ingredients:
- Butter flavored cooking spray
- 3 egg yolks, room temperature
- 2 eggs, room temperature
- 2 tbsp. powdered sugar
- ¼ cup honey
- 4 ½ tbsp. cake flour

Directions:
1. Place the rack in the cooking pot. Spray an 8-inch round baking dish with cooking spray and lightly coat with flour.
2. In a large bowl, beat egg yolks, eggs, and powdered sugar until combined.
3. In a small saucepan over medium heat, heat honey until it starts to simmer. Let simmer 2 minutes.
4. With mixer running, slowly beat in the hot honey. Beat mixture 8-10 minutes until pale and thick and doubled in size. Gently tap the bowl on the counter to remove any air bubbles.
5. Sift flour into mixture and gently fold in to combine. Pour the batter into the pan and tap again to remove air bubbles. Place the cake on the rack.
6. Add the tender-crisp lid and set to bake on 350°F. Bake the cake 15 minutes, center should still be soft.
7. Transfer to a wire rack and let cool in pan 30 minutes. Invert onto serving plate and serve.

Nutrition Info:
- InfoCalories 97,Total Fat 3g,Total Carbs14 g,Protein 3g,Sodium 23mg.

Strawberry Crumble

Servings: 5
Cooking Time: 2 Hours
Ingredients:
- 1 cup almond flour
- 2 tablespoons butter, melted
- 10 drops liquid stevia
- 4 cups fresh strawberries, hulled and sliced
- 1 tablespoon butter, chopped

Directions:
1. Lightly, grease the Ninja Foodi's insert.
2. In a suitable, stir in the flour, melted butter and stevia and mix until a crumbly mixture form.
3. In the pot of the prepared Ninja Foodi, place the strawberry slices and dot with chopped butter.
4. Spread the flour mixture on top evenly
5. Close the Ninja Foodi's lid with a crisping lid and select "Slow Cooker".
6. Set on "Low" for 2 hours.
7. Press the "Start/Stop" button to initiate cooking.
8. Place the pan onto a wire rack to cool slightly.
9. Serve warm.

Nutrition Info:
- InfoCalories: 233; Fats: 19.2g; Carbohydrates: 10.7g; Proteins: 0.7g

Cherry Cheesecake

Servings: 8
Cooking Time: 30 Minutes
Ingredients:
- 4 packages cream cheese, at room temperature
- 1 cup granulated sugar
- 3 tablespoons cornstarch
- 3 whole eggs
- 2 egg yolks
- ¼ cup heavy (whipping) cream
- 1 teaspoon kosher salt
- 1½ cups crushed graham crackers
- ½ cup unsalted butter, melted
- 1 cup water
- 1 can cherries in syrup

Directions:
1. In a large bowl, combine the cream cheese, sugar, cornstarch, eggs, egg yolks, cream, and salt. Use an electric mixer to mix until smooth and velvety.
2. In a medium bowl, combine the graham crackers and melted butter until it resembles wet sand.
3. Line the inside of the Ninja Multi-Purpose Pan or another 9-inch round baking dish with plastic wrap. Ensure the wrap is flush to the bottom of the dish and comes fully up the sides of the pan.
4. Place the graham cracker mixture in the center of the dish. Use a silicone-tipped spatula to press the mix outward. The mix should lay completely and evenly across the bottom of the dish.
5. Pour the cheesecake batter over the crust, then use the spatula to evenly smooth it out. Tightly wrap the top of the baking dish with a new piece of plastic wrap so that the cheesecake is completely covered.
6. Place the cheesecake on Reversible Rack, making sure it is in the lower steam position. Place rack with pan in pot. Pour the water into the pot. Assemble pressure lid, making sure the pressure release valve is in the SEAL position.
7. Select PRESSURE and set to HI. Set time to 30 minutes. Select START/STOP to begin.
8. When pressure cooking is complete, allow pressure to naturally release for 10 minutes. After 10 minutes, quick release remaining pressure by moving the pressure release valve to the VENT position. Carefully remove lid when unit has finished releasing pressure.
9. Remove top layer of plastic wrap from the cheesecake. Refrigerate the cheesecake to completely cool, at least 4 hours.
10. When ready to serve, remove the cheesecake from the refrigerator and place on a serving dish or cutting board. Use top edges of the remaining plastic wrap to remove cheesecake from the pan. Pull the plastic wrap out from underneath cheesecake. Top the cheesecake with the cherries in syrup as desired and serve.

Nutrition Info:
- InfoCalories: 789,Total Fat: 58g,Sodium: 760mg,Carbohydrates: 57g,Protein: 13g.

Gingery Chocolate Pudding

Servings: 4
Cooking Time: 20 Min

Ingredients:

- 2 oz. chocolate, coarsely chopped /60g
- 1 ½ cups of Water /375ml
- ¼ cup Cornstarch /32.5g
- 1 cup Almond Milk /250ml
- ¼ cup Sugar /32.5g
- 3 Eggs, separated into whites and yolks
- Zest and Juice from ½ Lime
- 2 tbsp Butter, softened /30g
- ½ tsp Ginger, caramelized /2.5g
- A pinch of Salt

Directions:

1. Combine together the sugar, cornstarch, salt, and softened butter, in a bowl. Mix in lime juice and grated lime zest. Add in the egg yolks, ginger, almond milk, and whisk to mix well.
2. Mix in egg whites. Pour this mixture into custard cups and cover with aluminium foil. Add 1 ½ cups or 375ml of water to the Foodi. Place a reversible rack into the Foodi, and lower the cups onto the rack.
3. Seal the pressure lid, choose Pressure, set to High, and set the time to 25 minutes. Press Start. Once the cooking is complete, do a quick pressure release. Carefully open the pressure lid, and stir in the chocolate. Serve chilled.

Cranberry Cheesecake

Servings: 8
Cooking Time: 1 Hr

Ingredients:

- 1/3 cup dried cranberries /44g
- 1 cup water /250ml
- ½ cup sugar /65g
- 1 cup coarsely crumbled cookies/ 130g
- 1 cup mascarpone cheese, room temperature /130g
- 2 eggs, room temperature
- 2 tbsp sour cream /30ml
- 2 tbsp butter, melted /30ml
- ½ tsp vanilla extract /2.5ml

Directions:

1. Fold a 20-inch piece of aluminum foil in half lengthwise twice and set on the pressure cooker. In a bowl, combine melted butter and crushed cookies; press firmly to the bottom and about 1/3 of the way up the sides of a 7-inch springform pan. Freeze the crust while the filling is being prepared.
2. In a separate bowl, beat together mascarpone cheese and sugar to obtain a smooth consistency; stir in vanilla extract and sour cream. Beat one egg and add into the cheese mixture to combine well; do the same with the second egg.
3. Stir cranberries into the filling. Transfer the filling into the crust. Into the pot, add water and set the reversible rack at the bottom. Center the springform pan onto the prepared foil sling. Use the sling to lower the pan onto the reversible rack.
4. Fold foil strips out of the way of the lid. Close the crisping lid and select Bake/Roast; adjust the temperature to 250°F or 122°C and the cook time to 40 minutes. Press Start.
5. When the time is up, open the lid and let to cool the cheesecake. When, transfer the cheesecake to a refrigerator for 2 hours or overnight.
6. Use a paring knife to run along the edges between the pan and cheesecake to remove the cheesecake and set to the plate.

Chocolate Mousse

Servings: 12
Cooking Time: 25 Minutes
Ingredients:
- Nonstick cooking spray
- 8 oz. semisweet chocolate chips
- 8 eggs, separated
- 1 teaspoon vanilla
- ¼ cup + 2 tbsp. powdered' sugar

Directions:
1. Spray an 8-inch springform pan with cooking spray. Line the bottom with parchment paper.
2. Melt the chocolate in a microwave safe bowl in 30 second intervals.
3. Beat the egg yolks until thick and pale. Slowly beat in the melted chocolate until combined. Fold in the vanilla.
4. Beat the egg whites with ¼ cup of sugar until soft peaks form. Fold ¼ of the egg whites into the chocolate mixture just until combined. Gently fold in remaining egg whites. Pour into the prepared pan.
5. Place the rack in the cooking pot and place the mousse on it. Add the tender-crisp lid and set to bake on 350°F. Bake 20-25 minutes until almost set, the mousse will still be a little jiggly in the middle.
6. Transfer mousse to a wire rack and let cool completely. Cover and refrigerate at least 4 hours. Dust with remaining sugar before serving.

Nutrition Info:
- InfoCalories 154,Total Fat 8g,Total Carbs 15g,Protein 5g,Sodium 48mg.

Gingerbread

Servings: 12
Cooking Time: 5 Hours
Ingredients:
- Butter flavored cooking spray
- 1½ cups self-rising flour
- ½ cup flour
- 1 tsp cinnamon
- ½ tsp fresh ginger, grated
- ¼ tsp allspice
- ¼ tsp salt
- 8 tbsp. butter, unsalted, soft
- 2/3 cup light molasses
- ¾ cup brown sugar
- 1 egg, beaten
- ½ cup skim milk
- ½ tsp baking soda

Directions:
1. Place the rack in the cooking pot. Spray and flour an 8-inch springform pan.
2. In a large bowl, combine both flours, spices, and salt.
3. Place butter, molasses, and brown sugar in a microwave safe bowl. Microwave on high until butter has melted, mix well.
4. Add butter mixture to dry ingredients and mix well.
5. Whisk in egg until combined.
6. In a measuring cup or small bowl, whisk together milk and baking soda. Add to batter and mix until blended.
7. Pour into prepared pan and place on the rack. Add the lid and set to slow cooking on high. Set timer for 5 hours. Gingerbread is done when it passes the toothpick test.
8. Carefully remove from cooking pot and let cool before cutting and serving.

Nutrition Info:
- InfoCalories 263,Total Fat 9g,Total Carbs 44g,Protein 3g,Sodium 183mg.

INDEX

A

Almond Quinoa Porridge 12
Apricot Snack Bars 35
Apricots With Honey Sauce 95
Artichoke Bites 32
Avocado Cups 19

B

Bacon & Sauerkraut With Apples 54
Bacon And Gruyère Egg Bites 15
Bacon Lime Chicken 40
Baked Eggs In Mushrooms 22
Barbecue Pork Ribs 50
Beef And Bell Pepper With Onion Sauce 58
Blackened Turkey Cutlets 47
Braised Lamb Shanks 59
Braised Short Ribs With Creamy Sauce 61
Breakfast Egg Pizza 23
Broccoli Turmeric Tots 29
Butter Pork Chops 53
Buttered Fish 72

C

Calzones With Sausage And Mozzarella 60
Caprese Stuffed Chicken 44
Caramel Walnut Brownies 96
Caramelized Cauliflower With Hazelnuts 30
Caramelized Salmon 64
Carrot Cake Muffins 22
Cauliflower Enchiladas 85
Char Siew Pork Ribs 51
Cheat Apple Pie 91
Cheese And Mushroom Tarts 85
Cheese Crusted Carrot Casserole 78
Cheesy Cauliflower Tater Tots 26
Cheesy Chilies 86
Cheesy Ham & Potato Casserole 52

Cheesy Spicy Pasta 87
Cherry Cheesecake 98
Cherry Pie 96
Chicken And Broccoli Stir-fry 38
Chicken Burrito Bowl 37
Chicken Chickpea Chili 39
Chicken Pasta With Pesto Sauce 41
Chicken Piccata 41
Chicken Stroganoff With Fetucini 42
Chicken With Bacon And Beans 44
Chicken With Cilantro Rice 46
Chicken With Mushroom Sauce 38
Chilaquiles 16
Chocolate Bread Pudding With Caramel Sauce 93
Chocolate Mousse 100
Chocolate Walnut Cake 92
Chorizo And Shrimp Boil 67
Chunky Pork Meatloaf With Mashed Potatoes 58
Churro Bites 89
Cinnamon Crumb Donuts 21
Cinnamon Roll Monkey Bread 19
Classic Crab Imperial 67
Coconut Cream "custard" Bars 88
Coconut Shrimp 66
Cod Cornflakes Nuggets 63
Coffee Cake 92
Crab Bisque 72
Crab Rangoon's 35
Cranberry Cheesecake 99
Cranberry Vanilla Oatmeal 15
Créme Brulee 88
Crispy Cheesy Straws 28
Crispy Roast Pork 56
Crumbed Sage Chicken Scallopini 36
Cuban Pork 62

D

Dark Chocolate Brownies 95
Dried Tomatoes 29

E

Egg Spinach Bites 16

F

French Dip Sandwiches 18

G

Gingerbread 100
Gingery Beef And Broccoli 55
Gingery Chocolate Pudding 99
Glazed Walnuts 34
Greek Beef Gyros 50
Green Squash Gruyere 84
Green Vegan Dip 34
Grilled Tofu Sandwich 87
Ground Beef Stuffed Empanadas 55

H

Hainanese Chicken 43
Ham & Broccoli Frittata 13
Ham, Ricotta & Zucchini Fritters 61
Hearty Breakfast Skillet 18
Herb Roasted Mixed Nuts 25
Herbed Cauliflower Fritters 24
Herby Chicken With Asparagus Sauce 43
Homemade Vanilla Yogurt 17
Honey Short Ribs With Rosemary Potatoes 53
Horseradish Roasted Carrots 28
Hot & Sour Soup 80

I

Indian Butter Chicken 45
Irish Cream Flan 91
Italian Spinach & Tomato Soup 77
Italian Turkey & Pasta Soup 46

J

Jalapeno Meatballs 33
Jalapeno Salsa 30

K

Kale-egg Frittata 17
Korean Cabbage Cups 51

L

Leeks And Carrots 79

M

Maple Dipped Kale 83
Mashed Broccoli With Cream Cheese 79
Mediterranean Quiche 14
Mexican Rice & Beans 31
Mini Chocolate Cheesecakes 93
Mini Turkey Loaves 42
Mongolian Beef 52
Moon Milk 97
Mussel Chowder With Oyster Crackers 68
Mustard And Apricot-glazed Salmon With Smashed Potatoes 66

N

Noodles With Tofu And Peanuts 78

O

One Pot Ham & Rice 57

P

Panko Crusted Cod 74
Paprika Hard-boiled Eggs 23
Parmesan Stuffed Mushrooms 33
Parsley Mashed Cauliflower 76
Peanut Butter Banana Baked Oatmeal 21
Penne All Arrabbiata With Seafood And Chorizo 69
Pepper Crusted Tri Tip Roast 59
Pepper Smothered Cod 65
Pepperoni Omelets 20
Poached Egg Heirloom Tomato 23
Pomegranate Radish Mix 79

Popcorn Chicken 24
Pork Pie 57
Portuguese Honey Cake 97
Pot Roast With Biscuits 49
Potato Samosas 27

Q

Quinoa Protein Bake 12

R

Raspberry Cheesecake 90
Red Beans And Rice 76
Riviera Chicken 47
Roasted Squash And Rice With Crispy Tofu 80
Rosemary Potato Fries 32

S

Salmon With Dill Chutney 73
Salmon With Dill Sauce 70
Salmon, Cashew & Kale Bowl 75
Sausage & Broccoli Frittata 20
Savory Custards With Ham And Cheese 14
Seafood Gumbo 65
Sesame Tuna Steaks 74
Shrimp Egg Rolls 63
Skinny Cheesesteaks 54
Slow Cooked Chicken In White Wine And Garlic 36
Southern Sweet Ham 56
Southwest Tofu Steaks 77
Spiced Poached Pears 94
Spiced Red Snapper 73
Spicy Chicken Wings. 45
Spicy Grilled Shrimp 71
Spinach Hummus 34
Steamed Artichokes With Lemon Aioli 82
Steamed Sea Bass With Turnips 69
Strawberry Crumble 98
Stuffed Mushrooms 81
Sweet & Spicy Shrimp 70
Sweet And Salty Bars 90
Sweet Potato Gratin 31

Sweet Potatoes & Fried Eggs 13

T

Tilapia & Tamari Garlic Mushrooms 71
Tomato Galette 84
Tuna Patties 75
Tuna Zoodle Bake 64
Turkey & Cabbage Enchiladas 48
Turkey & Squash Casserole 39
Turkey Croquettes 37
Turkey Green Chili 40

V

Vanilla Cheesecake 94
Veggie And Quinoa Stuffed Peppers 81
Veggie Potpie 82
Veggie Primavera 83

W

Whole Roasted Cabbage With White Wine Cream Sauce 86
Wrapped Asparagus In Bacon 27

Z

Zesty Brussels Sprouts With Raisins 26
Zucchini Muffins 25

Air Fry Roast Pork 180°C
25 mins per 500g
22 " " lb

Cooked y reaches
65°C / 145°F in thickest part

Lovefood Not looking
= Air fry Calculator

= 1.2kg 60mins.